WANDERMUST

A HERO'S JOURNEY TO SEVEN TRUTHS

MIKE GREEN
MASTER CERTIFIED COACH

Our deepest truths are found in the unknown.

Copyright © 2022 Mike Green.

All rights reserved. This book or any portion thereof may not be reproduced or used in any manner whatsoever without the express written permission of the publisher except for the use of brief quotations in a book review.

ISBN: 978-0-578-36909-9

Library of Congress Control Number: 2022903247

www.hoselbooks.com

www.mikegreenleadership.com

I dedicate this book to my two boys, Tennyson and Atlas. May you both really live, explore, thrive, and never yield. And while discovering the landscapes of the world and the people that inhabit them, may you remember that the greatest landscapes to discover in this life are inside you.

CONTENTS

Acknowledgements....................................... vii
Author's Note... xi
Introduction: To Those Who Contemplate Wonders & Marvels.. 1
Chapter 1: South America: Vision....................... 11
Chapter 2: North America: Courage...................... 29
Chapter 3: Europe: Integrity........................... 61
Chapter 4: Asia: Intention 93
Chapter 5: Antarctica: Emotional Intelligence/Awareness . 119
Chapter 6: New Zealand and Australia: Optimism 139
Chapter 7: Africa: Legacy 163
Afterword... 177
About the Author 179

ACKNOWLEDGEMENTS

Thank you, Mom, for mentoring kindness, taking care of others, and humor. You are pure sweetness. To my deceased father, thank you for modeling curiosity about people and their stories, places (especially places to eat), and the outdoors, and teaching me the value of bartering. Also for the weekend "work details." Because of these, I learned how to work hard, which has served me well.

To my wife, Erin. Through all of this book-writing process you have been patient and supportive. Even when I woke up at 4 a.m. to write or had to take a call in the middle of the weekend. Picking you up on the bus twelve years ago has been the greatest adventure of all. Each day is a gift. You are beautiful inside and out. You have taught me to slow down ("harness your energy"), enjoy the moment, and see the good in an untrained Hound. Thank you for putting up with me.

The book would not be what it is today without my editor, Robin Bethel. Robin's patience, keen eye for detail, and ability to get the best out of me was paramount to the success of this project. Stacy Ennis of Nonfiction Book School taught me the book-writing process, answered my emails, and reassured me throughout the process. I am grateful for the time, energy, and input my beta readers put forth. Thank you: Janice Prince, Polly

Porter Ells, Kristie Hannon, Catherine Fishman, Matt Lindsey, Matt Gilligan, Fred Dent, James Siller, Cory Lawrence, Marc "Mango" Magnus-Sharpe, and Steve Opat. Thank you, my hometown friend and indie publisher Michael McGruther of Hosel and Ferrule Books. Your support throughout the experience made all the difference. To my high school English teacher, Mr. Ron Quinlan, thank you for editing my first articles and encouraging me so many years ago. I raise my pint of Guinness in your memory and honor. To Justin Foster of Fosterthinking I am grateful for all your support and friendship. My deepest gratitude to my coach Jan Prince for the many years of asking great questions that have made all the difference.

To the good people of Hornell, New York: I am extremely proud of growing up in "an old railroad town in Western New York." I am grateful for all that Hornell afforded me. There are far too many Hornellians to thank here. I trust you know who you are and have a story to tell about our friendship. A special thank you to Walt, Robin, and Paul Randall for so many things. Especially helping me prepare "Kerouac: The Easy Riding Freedom Chariot of Adventure" for its maiden voyage to Alaska. A Montepulciano shout out to Father Jim Jeager. I believe you sent me cigars on every continent! Thank you to Barbara Coe and Robert Hunter. Your support and guidance in my early years of travel and "adult life" set me on the proper course. Fran and Lisa Marino, owners of Club 57 of Hornell, you always hired me when I returned from a global adventure. Thank you, Bill and Barb Castle of Pollywogg Holler. The Holler was a respite between adventures. Not to mention an amazing place to experience your global wisdom and homemade wine.

To my brothers of Grim Anarchic. Your actions throughout it all have been beyond words. My life has been enhanced because of you all. Enough said.

To the hundreds of friends around the world that always encouraged me "to write a book about your adventures," a heartfelt thank you. I have made good on my promise. I sincerely hope you enjoy it.

To my past, current, and future clients. Thank you for the honor and privilege of coaching you on your journey.

AUTHOR'S NOTE

The memories I've shared of my adventures across seven continents are real. While my memory isn't perfect and some dialogue has been recreated, everything remains true to the spirit of the moment, as I remember it. A metaphor that I thought about many times while writing this book was to get dragonflies of memories into one Ball canning jar in order as they happened. Like dragonflies, my memories fade and appear scattered, but brought together, I figured I could see them (and their glow) a bit better. And the metaphor helped. I feel I've captured them well.

Most names remain the same but a few have been changed. Ian Roundbail is a composite character based on real clients and our Adventure Coaching sessions in Alaska. Certain parts of his and my story included here have been changed for clarity and creative effect.

INTRODUCTION

To Those Who Contemplate Wonders and Marvels

"There is more to us than we know. If we can be made to see it, perhaps for the rest of our lives we will be unwilling to settle for less."

— Kurt Hahn,
Outward Bound Founder

"Clear left! Clear right!"

The helicopter's rotary engine starts, the rotors begin to spin, and a small whiff of fuel hits the cockpit.

This sound, sight, and smell. It takes me back across the world.

Crossing Iraq from one small forward operating base to another. Hitching a ride for a tahr hunt in New Zealand. Heading out to the drill ships in the Gulf of Mexico. Flying to the upper Clear Creek of Alaska for the leadership fishing adventure of a lifetime.

And now here I am in Alaska again, with another leadership coaching client who's ready for adventure—and transformation.

Ian Roundbail is in the front seat with the pilot, looking like a kid who just got a new toy. Ready to set out on this final leg of our leadership adventure coaching experience.

As he's been telling me throughout our coaching conversations, he's been working his ass off for fourteen years without doing anything for himself. Now he's ready to unplug, experience the wild of Alaska, and drop down into a deeper place in himself.

As he put it, he's at a critical point in his life and career, and realized if he stays on his same track, he'll soon burn out, lose the love he has for his work, and not even know his kids and wife. He knows he works way too much, often twelve-hour days, but can't seem to pull himself away. So he's here with me away from the noise of daily life to take inventory of what's really important. To find "the truths" as I call them, of what matters, and after that make a plan to live out those "truths." Because, as he's said, he can't keep living like he has been.

We've been working together for nine months, and this trip is both a continuation and zenith moment in our coaching journey.

The helicopter lifts off the pad and exposes the Nenana River, today a cold ash gray. As we head higher into the air, I see more of what the locals call "Glitter Gulch" shoved up against the entrance of Denali National Park and Preserve, and it's a long wash of memory and emotion. For over twenty years I've been exploring, working, hunting, guiding, instructing, and coaching across the terrain whisking by below.

As we continue to the east, the pilot asks me, "So you guided for big game around here?"

"Oh yeah," I answer. "Lots of memories in these mountains and valleys."

Ian stays quiet, absorbed in capturing the rugged beauty with his GoPro. The pilot nods and continues. "What did you hunt for?" he asks.

I give him the standard answer. "Moose, Dall sheep, caribou, wolves, and bear. Mostly on horseback."

"That sounds like quite the life," the pilot says.

I nod.

He's right, and I'm grateful.

As we continue in flight, I stay focused on, and excited for, Ian. Focused on his physical and emotional safety; excited for his continuing discoveries, in the wild of himself and the raw nature around us. He's been working hard on his "inward journey" and this experience is important to him. And to me, too, for that matter.

I've been doing these types of trips for years, and each time, it's like a homecoming. My clients usually feel my grounded ease. "You're calmer out here, Mike," is what I often hear.

The outdoors has a way of doing that if you let it. It constantly reminds you of what is important. Out here, I'm most myself, and that felt peace usually helps my clients risk a bit more themselves. And that's good. The quiet, beauty, and purity around us offers a lot and also demands something in return.

From the start Ian did a great job, meeting each experience with his whole self.

We'd just come back from sea kayaking in the Prince William Sound, where he was blown away by the beauty, size, and sound of the glaciers—like "cracking thunder," he'd mused. I'd made him a cup of tea during a break and left him for a half hour to take it all in alone. Thirty minutes later he came back shaken but doing his best to make a joke of the experience. "Fucking hell, Mike. Don't do that to me without giving me a heads-up. I got tears of joy or something. Shit is just falling off inside me like that glacier."

I can't say I was surprised.

His experience here is similar to those of my other clients. Excitement mixed with nervous anticipation—of bears behind every bush, getting stranded, starving, maybe a broken leg scenario where they have to say, "Go ahead, Mike. Save yourself." To be fair, they came here to be put to the test and stretch their limits. So a little nervousness is about right.

Ian's an emotionally intelligent CEO of an aerospace company in Boulder that makes "small satellites." He's a Brit and a father of two. He is not "rocking the dad bod." And he's cool enough to not ask constant giddy questions. Although I can tell he wants to. (And I sure as hell don't mind either way.) Like a number of other clients, Ian's a high performer who understands that the skill set that got him to where he is—while incredibly valuable—isn't enough to get him where he now needs to go next. So he hired me as a coach, to help him find, reinforce, test, and ultimately put into action his truths in life and within his professional career.

This "Adventure Coaching" session Ian signed up for is a deep dive away from the usual distractions. No direct reports, no emails, no cell service. This quiet tends to be the most terrifying "unknown" for my clients.

"What will I do without my cell phone?"

"What if my team needs me?"

Or, "What if, God forbid, something happens with my family?"

However, over time, they come to realize a journey like this—which takes them away but helps them discover their truths of self and leadership—will ultimately benefit family members and colleagues. The people in their lives tend to intuitively know this too.

This is the case for Ian as well. His wife is very supportive, and his colleagues are super stoked for him. And I appreciate that—it helps him immerse in the experience.

I know the level of support on the outside will support his work on the inside.

It's a fact that we all need support, especially for our biggest explorations. People who help point us toward the path and people who help us along the journey.

Since I can remember, I've wanted to explore. I grew up in western New York, and it started close to home—in the woods out back or up in the hills in the long Canisteo Valley below our house. You couldn't keep me in one place for too long. But that drive to explore didn't give me a vision for the future until I discovered Ibn Battuta.

Battuta was a fourteenth-century Berber Muslim scholar and traveler from Tangier, Morocco. He was also the author of a book titled *The Rihla: A Gift to Those Who Contemplate the Wonders of Cities and the Marvels of Traveling*.

When I came across this title in early high school, I knew I had to read it. And when I did, a subtle and not-so-subtle excitement came over me, my soul, my being. Hell, I was in my teens. I didn't know what the feeling was—I couldn't articulate it. But I knew something changed. A strange sense of self was ignited. A sense that I, too, would travel the world. A knowing but not knowing how. Or a vision without really seeing anything. It was as if Ibn Battuta himself said to me those famous opening lines from his book: "I set out alone, having neither fellow-traveler in whose companionship I might find cheer, nor caravan whose part I might join, but swayed by an overmastering impulse within me and a desire long-cherished in my bosom to visit these illustrious sanctuaries. So, I braced my resolution to quit my dear ones, female and male, and forsook my home as birds forsake their nests."

I knew I was different from reading his book, and at the same time, I went on living my teenage years of wrestling, football, keg parties, chasing girls, and being a good kid who was known to work hard, get average grades, and be a bit "goofy." Then in my senior year of high school, I saw an Outward Bound brochure on a friend's dining room table.

The Outward Bound School is distinguished by training *through* rather than *for*. The sea, mountains, and desert landscapes where the courses take place, in tandem with Outward Bound principles, teach the hard, technical skills necessary for outdoor survival and also teach character. Since its founding in 1941, the program has evolved but never departed from creator Kurt Hahn's original concept—an intense experience surmounting challenges in a natural setting, which helps the individual build their sense of self-worth, helps the group come to a heightened awareness of human interdependence, and helps all grow in concern for those in danger and need.

Enough of this got conveyed on the brochure that as I read it, I thought, *I've got to do this!* Then I made it to the last page and saw the cost. My heart sank. I knew there was no way my parents could afford it.

I sheepishly showed my mom the brochure, not wanting to make her sad she and my dad couldn't afford something I wanted so much. She was quiet as she looked it over, and then mentioned something I hadn't noticed—that they offered financial aid. She talked to my dad about it and we sent the application in about a week later.

I was psyched to find out I was approved for financial aid and we would only need to pay a partial payment. My parents agreed they would pay for it if I worked for the plane fare. Which I did.

When I arrived at the Voyageur Outward Bound School in Ely, Minnesota, it was cold—really cold—and I loved the physical tests of endurance in the record-breaking winter ice and snow. As I learned winter camping skills, how to mush, and how to push through my exhaustion, I also learned a new level of strength and self-awareness. And I came to a deeper respect for the Four Pillars of Outward Bound: self-reliance, physical fitness, craftsmanship, and compassion. They made sense to me, I identified with them, and the experience I was having reinforced that I was good at them. My instructors, who traveled and adventured through various seasons of the year, also introduced me to the concept of "seasonal work–life balance." That you didn't have to automatically live a lifetime of nine-to-five with just two weeks off for yourself each year.

I was struck dumb with excitement. At the same time, I had my own excuses why I couldn't do it. It didn't jive with the work I'd been moving toward for years—being a K9 police officer. That wasn't a job you could do seasonally.

Yet even as I made my excuses, something started inside me.

After graduating from high school, I still got my criminal justice associate's degree, but I was beginning to question if I really did want to be a K9 officer after all.

Then as I waited to start at the police academy, I got a job as an orderly in a 125-bed hospital in my hometown. It was a great job. I really enjoyed the life, death, happiness, and drama that came with it, as patients welcomed me into their rooms to break up the boredom.

One patient in particular was able to help me put more pieces of that Ibn Battuta global travel puzzle into place. Before I met him, I'd just learned of a "wilderness rehabilitation/recovery program" for youth with addiction issues, which offered internships with a $100/month stipend. I couldn't get the thing out of my head—it was a way to actually start living the seasonal work–life balance that had called to me years before. But the pay wasn't exactly promising. Moreover, when I looked into it, it seemed they'd most likely filled all the available slots.

Then at the hospital I met a ninety-two-year-old man having his prostate removed. He was bright, spry, and full of wisdom. And so one day, while irrigating his catheter, I asked him, "What is your secret to a full and healthy life?"

He answered me right away in a centered and grounded tone of voice. "Live with no regrets."

I paused, taken aback not by what he said, but how he said it. It felt like his words were meant directly for me, preparing me for something that was coming. I finished with the procedure and cleaned up while continuing small talk. I was still thinking over and processing his tone. Thinking about how certain he sounded in what he said, and that it was a gift of experience I shouldn't take lightly. Mainly because of how it affected me when I heard it. The feeling was strangely familiar, but I couldn't integrate it fully right then. Soon, though, it would change the trajectory of my life.

Two days later and two days before Thanksgiving, I got the call from the Wilderness Recovery Program operations manager. The person slated to start December 1 had to cancel, and he asked me how serious I was about "driving out there and starting anytime," as I'd told him before.

I was shocked. Dumbfounded. And at a loss for words. But after a few days of internal debate—the ridiculousness of some guy known for his parties to move out west and take a job making no money helping kids learn wilderness survival skills as part of their twelve-step program—I knew what to say. I knew I had to live with no regrets.

When it came time to go, though, I almost didn't make it. The morning after my going-away party, I was a blubbering mess and didn't want to leave town. Thankfully, my friends gave me the support I needed at the time. They essentially threw me in the car and told me not to come back. So, with a car full of junk and one mountain bike, I cried my way west.

From there, I'd go on to work in wilderness programs in Maryland, then Florida, then Russia, all of which set me on a path around the globe. All leading me to the work I do now, and to this moment in a helicopter high in the Alaskan sky.

After three decades crossing the globe and discovering my own truths, now I help others find the life and leadership truths they're meant to live out. Sometimes they intersect with mine and sometimes they're all their own. The point isn't to arrive at any specific truth, just at the ones that rise from inside, are connected to your deepest core, and are discovered through your own reflection and experience. The truths that you find when you open into the unknown.

These are the truths that—however simple they may sound—change your life.

Ian's voice rings out over the intercom. "Mike, are we hiking those mountains below us?"

I laugh. "No. Way too crazy. We're hiking through the valley to our left. Almost there."

We come into a long valley running east to west, framed on all sides by mountains of various sizes. I point to one of them. "That peak to our far left just jutting out—that's Egil's Knob, named after my Norwegian friend and legendary hunting guide. I proposed to my wife, Erin, on that mountain."

We continue to descend into the valley and look around us. Large expanses of land stretch to the south and west, and more extends beyond the cook shack to the east.

I continue to see the ghosts of my past on the horse trails below. Right now, the camp is empty of horses, hunters, and help. However, it holds holograms ten plus years of me guiding this area.

Ian is impressed with how unimpressive the camp looks. "Wow. I thought it would be a lodge like on TV."

I laugh. "You soon find that this place is a palace if or when the cold rain comes."

The helicopter lands, the rotors stop spinning, we get out, and we unload. When we're done, the pilot starts the engine again, and as the helicopter heads up and over and out of the valley, Ian gets quiet. Real quiet.

"We are way out here," he says.

"Yep," I respond. "We are way out here. But being way out here will get you back to where you want to go. Back to who you really are, were, or choose to be."

"Fuck, that is poetic," he says, in his very British accent.

"If you're lucky, you'll find that it's also true."

That's exactly what happened to me when I left New York in my Mazda 626. My friends helped me cut the cord of familiarity and safety, and it made all the difference.

And now I help others do the same.

I head toward the cook shack to begin opening it up.

CHAPTER 1

South America: Vision

It doesn't take long to remove the "bear proof" window shutters, sweep out the dust, and prepare the water jugs. Now we can start to settle in.

I hand Ian a folding chair and ask him to go find a spot outside facing the highest peak. Then I rummage around until I find the map and compass above the door, in an old wooden oil can box. I bring them out along with a chair, some homemade jerky, a bottle of scotch, water, and my pipe tobacco—I'm hungry and ready for a smoke.

Once I sit, I spread out the map and hand Ian the compass.

"What is it now?" he quips. "Map and compass class?" He grabs the bag of jerky and picks out a piece to gnaw on for a bit.

"Yep," I answer. "It's time to understand where we are and where we want to go. Not to mention where you are, out in the wilds of your own life, and where you want to go after you're done with this journey. Your own hero's journey. So we're going to sit with vision for a while."

Ian laughs and says, "Ah, come on, Mike, can we just learn

about the map and not go into a deep conversation? I just got here an hour ago. Let me enjoy this place a bit before you start getting me into my head. At least let me finish this piece of awesome jerky."

As I orientate the map, I laugh. "Man, you are so sensitive. I'm just asking you to think about a few things. Where you currently are—'the known world,' in Joseph Campbell terms. And where you want to go, called the 'unknown world.' That unknown world is both a vision and a destination, and also a journey you have to move through once we go back home.

"What we're about to do in the next couple of days can be a metaphor for mapping out or scoping your known world. Getting a clearer sense of what's working, what you want to continue, and then also what isn't working and what you don't want to continue." I lift up the paper in my hand. "The map is not the destination. It's only a representation of what's in front of you. But we use it to hold a vision of our destination. The compass helps you plot your course and move across it. It also helps keep you on track."

Ian rolls his eyes and grabs another piece of jerky, as I open up the pipe tobacco kit and set it up for a proper smoke. My pipe is a meerschaum corncob pipe, just like General MacArthur used.

"God, Mike, this map and compass metaphor is good but come on, man, we just got here."

I raise my eyebrows. "What, so you wanna wait another ten years?"

He smiles. "Fine, okay. We'll talk about it. Let me guess, the map represents my life, the compass represents 'my truths.' Correct?"

Ian rushes forward. "So Mike, I'm to figure out what my life map is, decide on a destination or vision of what I want in life, and use my newly discovered or current truths as 'a compass'"— his fingers reach up and mark air quotes—"to make a route or plan to reach that destination."

"You are a quick learner, my friend," I say, as I uncover my pipe.

"Getting comfortable, I see," he says. "How long is this class going to go on for here?"

I laugh as I pack the pipe. "As long as it takes, Ian. I am packing patience."

He shakes his head and smiles.

After I light my pipe, I begin to teach him the high-level points of orienteering, which is a fancy term for map and compass skills. He's a quick learner and asks a lot of questions.

Eventually, our talk winds down and we simply sit quietly in the Alaska sun. As Ian continues to study the map and think about the vision he holds for his life, I become thoughtful, as I often do when I smoke my pipe. I watch the smoke drift toward the "moose bog" that butts up against the small hills to the west. Moose like that area because the bogginess provides a consistent, rich food source. But I hate it. It's hard to walk in or even around.

My mind drifts like the pipe smoke, back to a time much like now, when I was teaching the basics of map and compass in the wide open space of Ecuador on the "Trek de Condor." The "trek" was much like hiking through the moose bog here—wet, tiresome, and frustrating. And vision came to the forefront then, too. Deep in the bog of the trek, it was essential to keep the group going forward.

I'd been exploring Mexico and Central America for about four months, with the intent to learn all things cigars, when I stopped in at the Costa Rica Rainforest Outward Bound School (CRROBS), based in Manuel Antonio on the west coast.

My experience and skill set as an Outward Bound alumni and

wilderness instructor in various programs afforded me opportunities to visit and work at Outward Bound Schools around the world. As I traveled, I would reach out to the local program manager, tell them who I was and where I'd worked, then ask if I could stop by and support their program. All of them said yes. I did the same in Costa Rica, and soon was asked to lead their upcoming eighty-five-day university semester course that would span three countries: Costa Rica, Ecuador, and Peru.

The course would provide opportunities for students to gain real wilderness skills along with developing decision-making, problem solving, leadership, and teamwork. As the trip progressed, students would have increasing responsibility that culminated in their planning, coordinating, and executing the final expedition in Peru. It sounded amazing.

I jumped at the opportunity—and thank God.

Costa Rica was a damn banquet. We traveled from the east coast to the west coast using "campesino trails" crossing the Pan-American Highway, something we were told had never been done before in the program. We spent twenty-four glorious days surfing, rafting, kayaking, and, of course, orienteering, while surrounded by pristine beauty.

Then we started our next adventure—the eight-day Trek de Condor, starting at El Tambo and ultimately taking us to the base and then top of Cotopaxi.

At 19,347 feet tall, Cotopaxi is the second-highest peak in Ecuador and one of the world's highest volcanos. And while all of Costa Rica, Ecuador, and Peru were incredible experiences, it was the coupled experience of the Trek de Condor and ascending to the glaciated top of Cotopaxi with my students that lit up my truth of vision.

First, though, it started with a heap of pain.

When we landed in Quito, Ecuador, I had an acute sinus

infection that at the elevation of 9,350 feet felt like two nails were being driven into my head.

Seth, one of my students, walked over to stand by me at baggage claim.

"Hey, Graceland, you going to be OK?" he asked. (The students gave me that nickname in Costa Rica because I wore gold Elvis sunglasses as we traveled the country. How could I not? They looked great.)

I winced, but said, "Yeah. Just help keep an eye on everyone for me." Seth, being dependable and a natural leader, replied, "I'm on it."

As I sat in a hard plastic chair waiting for the luggage and politely saying no to the peddlers of Coca-Cola in a bag, I watched my group work together to get the bags off the conveyor. They were a good group. Diverse as hell, hardworking, smart, capable, young, and fun. Though they could be difficult and clueless at times.

There was "Trucks" from San Fran, a determined redhead who never gave up. While crossing Costa Rica with a heavy backpack on her back and a machete in her hand, she must have fallen down a hundred times in one day. But she just kept on pushing through. Then there was Seth, a highly intelligent CU Boulder student. He was a mix of frat boy and unique individual. And he could be counted on. Haver was a good guy, but he'd just finished an expedition course earlier in the year and kept comparing our experience with his last. Somewhere on the east side of the Costa Rica mountains, huge blisters finally tempered his know-it-all attitude and we all started to like him a lot more. Erika was—and looked like—the daughter of a museum curator. She was strong, funny, and a (Canadian) voice of reason. Brandon—also known as "Neckbeard Boy" for the massive growth of whiskers from his chin to his chest, he was a funny, intelligent, able guy who seemed a mix of everything all at once. Megan was also funny and able, and someone we all gravitated toward. Matt came across at first just as a "stoner"; however, I soon learned he was also introspective and deep. Chris was from NYC and a dancer. Being the oldest out of all of us, he brought a different perspective to the group.

By the time we landed in Quito we were a great team that worked well together and supported each other. We were used to the early mornings, camp chores, and going to bed more exhausted than the night before. We knew all too well everyone's body functions, and we were used to seeing everyone wear the same dirty clothes. We knew many of the secrets we wouldn't tell our friends in our hometowns, and we all loved to laugh. We didn't have "cliques" within our group. We genuinely cared about each other.

That wasn't to say we wanted to be around each other all the time. We sure as hell didn't. But the great thing about traveling Costa Rica on a campesino trail with a machete in your hands is that you've got an outlet for frustrations. So let them out we did, and overall, I was proud of everyone. We had just accomplished something that, according to the Outward Bound program manager and the mountain campesinos, had never been done before. The campesinos would ask us, "Where are you hoping to go?" And when we would answer, "To the Pacific Ocean," all of them would clutch at their hearts and exclaim, "By the blood of Christ!" But we did it.

The group rejoiced that all our bags had made the flight, and after we made it to the hostel, we had a lazy morning with a basic breakfast. Midmorning, we were briefed by Mark and John of our "Ecuador Trekking/Mountaineering Section." John continued on with us, and we started our day hike and overnight along the Oyacachi River.

The air was moist and the ground was full of soft mud that would suck off your boots. Our progress was slow and surprisingly difficult due to the mud. We also stopped several times to admire various rock paths dating back to the time of the Inca and to explore the random ancient stone structures and carvings.

The cable crossing across the river was easy for us, having already done crossings like it several times in Costa Rica. That success gave our group a win for the day and ultimately a shot of energy to finish strong at the end of the hike. We eventually arrived at our home for the night—each of us tired, muddy, wet, and smelling like Ecuadorian peat and cow shit. We ate heartily, relaxed, and slept well.

The next day we woke up early in a half-asleep stupor to put on half-dry gear and socks (always a pleasure). We crossed more fallen bridges and cable crossings and trekked through forests and farmlands, later remarking that the hard trail conditions were a barrier for the faint of heart. But our reward for pushing through was stopping to eat with the Quechan people, a true cultural experience. We even got to eat guinea pig! I was in heaven. I just wished I had a cigar to enhance the experience.

We found a place to sleep and the next day started early, hitching a ride with a wide-eyed local milk truck driver to the beginning of the Trek de Condor. We all put on layers to fight off the cold and rain gear to protect our precious dry clothes and skin. Yet we knew being dry was a fleeting condition. And we knew things were going to get harder.

Before taking off, we took some time to set our vision and unite around our shared goal to summit Cotopaxi. Then we went back over basic orienteering skills—how to "orient" the map, what the lines (or contours) mean both close and far apart, where we were, and where we were going.

A group needs a map, compass, and an understanding of the

current state. Basically, an honest orientation of what is working and what is not, strengths, and opportunities—so you can say with certainty: we are here. With our vision and the help of the map, we'd be able to make informed decisions on our best courses of action. We could also orient our strengths, responsibilities, duties, and schedule. The map allowed everyone to understand where we were on the journey, and mentally prepare for potential rough spots.

Then, John and I explained that as essential as the map was, it wasn't the reality of our trek. That understanding the map and how to use the compass would always keep us moving toward our goal, but that the terrain, weather, emotions, and ability to see our goal would always change. We talked about how our strengths and our limitations would be out for everyone to see and experience—it would be a challenge. And that in order to reach our individual goals and collective goal of reaching the summit of Cotopaxi, everyone would need to play their part. While standing there at the trailhead mostly fed, dry, and happy, the mood was, "OK. We got this."

Next, we discussed the high-level plan for the next five to six days. We would hike, get dirty, lose our boots in trail-sucking mud, pass tourist trains of horses or llamas, camp where we could, get rained on and snowed on. Hopefully we would be able to dry our clothes every so often. Once we got to the base of Cotopaxi, another plan would be made. Pretty simple yet full of possibilities. With the immediate plan laid out, questions answered, and cloud cover coming in, we took our first steps toward Cotopaxi and last steps on "firm ground." The rest was a trudge in the mud.

As we progressed throughout the day, John and I hung back and watched the group use the tools we'd reintroduced them to earlier.

Orienteering is a great activity to teach or reinforce the importance of vision within a group. When you're just learning the skill, you are mostly learning perspective. If you're able to triangulate from your point to two other points of reference (thus making a triangle) you can pretty much get a good understanding of where you are on the map (assuming you've first oriented the map to the north). Once that's complete you can begin to put together or translate what the contour lines look like in the form of terrain or land characteristics. Mainly, lines that are close together mean the land is steep or characteristics of the land are steep. Circles inside circles represent hills or mountains.

The objective of orienteering is to find the best way from point A to point B, and John and I knew our group of seasoned Outward Bound students had a good foundation for success, which would be helped along by some basic trial and error. However, we also knew the low cloud cover high in the Andes Mountains can make it very difficult, stressful, and intense for any group. Let alone for those just learning orienteering. Add on the conditions of the terrain and levels of exhaustion, patience, hunger, cold, and just a general "sick of this shit and you people" attitude, and it becomes a steep learning curve for all involved.

We continued to slosh through the various consistencies of mud, sometimes having to fight the mud for one of our rubber boots while standing on one foot balancing to get it out. At first you would hear laughter and a joke or two. Soon, though, it became a curse and a groan.

Of course, the real rain of the day started just as we began making lunch. Nothing like soggy tuna fish and pita bread with a side of mustard to keep you going. Then just as fast as it came in, the rain ended, and out of nowhere sunlight bathed us, the valley, and the mud all around us. A rookie hiker would quickly take off their poncho. However, our seasoned group knew to let the sun dry them first so we could pack them away responsibly dry.

Situational awareness is something Mother Nature teaches you in the outdoors. If you pay attention, you can often prepare for a storm with hints that feel simultaneously vague and also powerful. Alex noticed it first. "Weather seems to be coming down that mountainside heading right for us." He convinced the group to work fast and efficiently to get camp set up before that weather arrived.

Nearby our campsite was a group of French "tourists"—I say tourists because they had llamas carry all their kit. We all watched them work together to make camp. Some helped, some didn't. Some helping worked hard, others didn't. The "guide" saw the weather coming in. You could tell because he was talking loud and moving fast. But this only made those working hard with him work faster in an ineffective manner. And the rest seemed to just drink more as they sat on their asses, having accomplished a couple "camp chores" (the cook tent up, kitchen lined out, and one or two tents starting to be erected). As the French tourists realized that bad weather was about to hit them, they quickly ran to their backpacks and pulled out rain gear. This produced a "yard sale" of clothes and gear scattered throughout their camp. They had no team cohesion, no systems, and no real leadership or vision. We never saw the result because we all headed to our tents.

The weather Alex predicted arrived in force. First the wind, which was cold—cold enough you knew it was going to be followed with rain. Which it was. The rain came in torrents and didn't let up. Eventually, two of our students emerged from their tents to make dinner for everyone and deliver the meals to the tents so the others didn't have to get wet. True servant leadership. After eating, we talked between the tents until we were asleep. The cold rain and soon-to-be snow made for great sleeping weather.

Waking up the next day, thankfully to no "real" rain, we ate something warm and drank coffee while checking out the entire valley and the snowcapped mountains in the distance. Our "map person of the day"—we rotated jobs daily—spent some time orienteering, and then we were off.

We put our dried feet into our moist socks and dank rubber boots and started climbing. It was a gradual increase in elevation but still we began to notice the first stages of altitude sickness at lunch. Having leftover food and requests for aspirin were sure signs.

The rain grew heavier, and when it hit its afternoon peak, we found an old "chosa" (a plantation shed) that had been vacant for years. There were four sheds connected to each other, three of them covered with bird shit and the fourth with bird shit and a dead, mostly decomposed horse. This would be home for the night. The rain having thoroughly soaked our ponchos and clothes and washed away our determination to keep going through the rain, the bird shit seemed manageable.

The next morning started out with sun and excellent views of Cotopaxi, Antisana, and Sincholahua, which helped boost our motivation to once again start trudging through the marshy valley. As we marveled at the beauty, the students bantered back and forth about the best route options available to the naked eye. In time our view of the mountains was obstructed by the weather coming in, which the students noticed and said we should prepare for. I was proud when they noticed it. We decided to "double-time it" to our campsite as it rained and hailed. It was miserable. But we moved forward.

John and I knew that this is where individuals or a group can either falter or rise to the occasion. And by agreeing to the physical challenge of hiking double time to our campsite, they had given themselves something to focus on, helping us in this instance rise. We made good time and arrived at camp about two hours before dark.

We put up our tents, ate quickly, and decided that's where we'd stay to experience the rain and snow. We woke up the next day slow, tired, and wet. Nothing sucks more than having to pack wet gear, but we did.

We headed out through a marshy valley and up a ridge near Sincholaqua, then skirted around Chico. In the distance we could see the weather starting to clear and we got some magnificent views of the snowcapped peaks around us.

In quick time we would be finishing the trek and starting the next phase leading us into ascending the peak. We would also soon have the chance to sleep inside a walled structure called "the Refugio," on the other side of Cotopaxi approximately three thousand feet below the summit. First, though, we spent a moment taking it all in. This vista would be part of our fuel.

When we made it to the Refugio, we finished off the evening with dinner, a plan for tomorrow's training, and preparations for tomorrow night's midnight ascent. Everyone would be attempting the trip except for Brandon, who was having gastro issues.

We went to lie in our beds only to pretend to sleep, as we listened to about 120-plus people either getting ready to do their midnight ascents or returning from their summit adventures. The next morning, we all stayed in bed for a while—with a book, a journal, or simply our own thoughts. Then we ate pancakes, told stories, and got ready to go outside. We had training to do.

John and I worked with some hired local guides (who would be supporting our group in our ascent) to get everyone lined out with gear—crampons to walk on ice and hard-packed snow, ice axes, and harnesses. We then practiced using our ice axes during a drill of "self-arresting" as you slide at mock speed down the side of the mountain. It was serious business, but we made it a fun experience. Basically, a nervous type of fun. We also learned how to "step" (forward and sideways) in the metal crampons. "Step, step, breathe, breathe." Having a little bit of time before dark, we did a quick snow shoveling avalanche course, so the group could see the different "morphologies" of snow and understand how certain snow can literally act as ball bearings for heavier layers of snow on top of it. With that completed we went inside the packed Refugio to eat dinner and try to get some sleep before 11:30 p.m. came.

We ate, did our final briefing, and left everyone to get their gear ready or "go to bed," if they could sleep over the buzz of movement, talking, and nervous energy running through the place. People packed their backpacks once, twice, or three times, each time focused on one thing or a specific task only to then forget if they packed something else. This happens when each piece of gear really counts. And it's magnified by the amount of nervousness within a person's mind and body.

I laid in bed half-dreaming, half-listening to the buzz of the room, a multilanguage soundtrack to our experience waiting. At 10:30, I quietly rose from bed, dressed, and put on a necklace with a silver cigar tube taped to it. Inside was a cigar I'd cut earlier that night, which I would keep warm against my body so that when I got to the summit, I could smoke it. Then I slipped on my boots and went outside.

The vibrant cold pierced me first. Then the brightness of the full moon and clear sky snapped me to full attention. It was majestic. The snow glistened silver, and small radiant beads of light sparkled up to the top of the summit. Hell, the whole mountain and surrounding mountains were "out" in all their glory. No clouds to cover them.

As I breathed in the frosted air I suddenly realized I was alone outside—the first time in many weeks that I was really alone.

It was just me and the shining summit of Cotopaxi. My goal. Our goal.

This vision, literally before me in all its incredible power and beauty, was what was holding us together through the slog and wet and bird shit. Our vision to reach the top of this mountain is what had kept us focused and motivated to keep moving. And it would be what kept us going—we weren't done yet. The hardest part was still to come.

Seeing Cotopaxi in the clear sky the night we set out was a brilliant reminder of the lifelong achievement we were reaching for. My responsibility as a leader would be to keep this vision and what it represented in front of each person in the group, whether we could see it directly ahead of us in any given moment or not.

Another part of my responsibility as a leader was considering the question—from where to lead? Sometimes it's best from out in front, sometimes in the middle, and sometimes from the back. It's essential a leader know how to best support a group's movement forward, taking into account group dynamics and also knowing their own limits and acting accordingly. Beyond helping everyone reach the goal, this also shows that people's safety—their mental and physical health—is above a leader's ego. In our case, it meant bringing in more experts, professional local mountaineers to help us complete the ascent. As I continued to stare at the summit, I was thankful we'd have their expertise. And of course, John's immutable childlike positive energy helped us all.

I noticed cold air seeping into my boots, reminding me I hadn't laced them up yet. I bent down and tied the laces, like I'd done thousands of times before. But this time felt different. I felt it in the air and in myself.

When the boots were laced up, I felt the support—that squeeze around the sides and top of my foot and ankles—in a new way. I felt deeply certain, confident, and able within my mind, body, and spirit. I've never forgotten that moment and often I go back to it when I need to feel the certainty, confidence, and deep capability within me. I remember the cold, naked summit, and the silver sparkling landscape, and a very calm, sure, confident feeling comes over me.

After a moment, I went inside to wait with my group. We would be the first ones up the mountain tonight.

When it was go time, we first broke into our three smaller groups, each one led by a mountaineer guide, one of whom was John. The idea was to move as a single body, but in three teams. If someone had to turn back, they would be taken down with one of the mountaineers and the other members of that group would attach themselves to the remaining groups. Then we started our ascent.

We knew the value of getting out of the Refugio first would be it just being us out there, on the ascent up at least. And we moved quickly for a while. I felt strong and sure with each step. My group was the first in the line of three, and we moved up the mountain with a good consistent pace.

We stopped often to catch our breath, which allowed us to also drop into the stillness. A stillness so thick you could almost lean on it.

The beauty was something that struck us dumb. Words could not describe it then or now.

As we climbed, a strange feeling came over me, an awareness that this was far beyond the capacity of language, senses, and euphoria. The lack of color paired with the sparkle of moonlight on white snow was something out of science fiction. I was overwhelmed with the awestruck sense of being so small in the grand gray landscape that glistened above me, at eye level, at my feet, and far below.

We were doing it. All our hard work was getting us to the summit.

For some in our group the experience was so powerful they had to step off the path to take a shit. A couple students (who will go unnamed) relieved their bowels while being roped in together and simultaneously leaning over their ice axes. They were both smiling, their asses facing downhill, their eyes uphill, laughing at the glory of the situation.

Two in our full group had to go back, but most of us made it to the summit. And since we were quite a bit ahead of other groups of climbers, we had twenty minutes or so to get group pictures, stare this way and that, and admire what was before us. Admire what we'd done. Cry, and be silent.

We'd reached the goal, and it was important everyone have time and space to enjoy the experience. To internalize the relationship of meeting and overcoming the challenge, in their own way.

We were transfixed. The full moon was above us, creating a stark black on the exposed rocks and creating gray shadows throughout the landscape. The contrast of white snow was so real, different, or amazing it created neural pathways in my brain, which I would later be reminded of when I experienced "shrooms" for the first time. This contrast was, for all of us, a memory we would never forget.

Our vision of completing the Trek de Condor and reaching this summit had sometimes been directly in front of us in its full visual glory and sometimes appeared as just a bunch of tight circles on the map. Either way, whether we could see the summit with our eyes or not, the goal was always there before us. And we all needed it to keep going.

In the moonlight and glory of our collective achievement, I pulled out the silver cigar tube from deep in my layers. I quickly opened the tube, took out the cigar, and lit it up.

"We realized our vision," I said quietly, with a puff. "And now we savor the moment."

CHAPTER 2

North America: Courage

THE SQUIRRELS UNDERNEATH the bunkhouse start to chirp and it shakes Ian and me out of our reverie. And I know it's time to come back to the moment.

I remember the bottle of scotch beside me and get up to go inside for some glasses.

Ian watches as I remove the logs and small glass jars filled with Pine-Sol that sit in front of the door. Then I open the door, careful to avoid the sixteen penny nails sticking out of it.

He shakes his head. "All this to keep a bear out, Mike? They must be some determined animals."

I laugh and disappear inside. "Yep, bears are big, strong, and determined for sure," I call behind me.

"And here we are sitting outside with our little cans of pepper spray," he says wryly.

As I come back out with the glasses, Ian nods toward the door and asks, "Does all that actually work?"

"Hard to tell!" I smile, kick over a large piece of wood to act as a table, set down the glasses, and fill them halfway. "It has up to this point, though."

"Christ." He reaches for his glass and laughs.

"What are you whingeing about, Ian?" I ask, happy to show off some of my new British slang. "If we see any bears, they'll have me to deal with."

"True. But still—" He raises his glass. "Here is to seeing no big, strong, determined bears."

I raise mine. "Big, strong, determined bears or not—here is to being in the moment. Which I believe takes courage."

Ian sips his scotch pensively. He looks at me, then the airstrip, and finally up to the mountains. As he settles in his chair, he extends his legs and lets out a sigh. "Courage," he says quietly. We sit in the sun, angled out in slightly different directions, but still taking in the same awesome landscape. Ian takes another sip and adds, "Alright, Mike, tell me. What's courage got to do with being in the moment?"

I put my glass down and lean forward. "Well, like right now. Here. It takes courage to take in your experience as it's happening and not control the hell out of it. To have vision, yeah, but not always feel you have to plan out every move a day or two ahead. To sit back and be out here in the bush, out of your comfort zone, with some trust. It takes a lot of courage to say, 'Yes, Mike, I trust you to guide me in the bush.'"

"Yeah, I feel that. Parts don't come easy."

"And it also takes courage to let go of distractions. I mean, there's a reason why distractions keep much of the world occupied—it's comfortable. And giving up the anesthesia can be scary. But it's worth it, because when you strip away the rest and be in the moment with yourself, you access inner resources and knowledge you didn't know existed. Or didn't let yourself fully connect to. And you find what really matters. Have you felt that this trip?"

Ian's eyes stay on the mountains. "Yes, I've felt that, too."

"Most people just stay in the control and distractions. They don't have the courage to enter into the moment with their experience and themselves in a real way, in the wild, and see what truths they find. Some distractions keep people distracted forever. And they never find their truths."

I watch the squirrels wrestling across the airstrip. "It's not like every single moment out here is magic. But at some point, when you stay in the moment, atop a mountain or sitting in the breeze or running from a bear or whatever—all distractions fall away and it gets clear. You claim the truth that's always been buried in there. And then you're ready to bring it back with you." I pour out more scotch. "That all starts with courage. You need courage to step into the unknown world."

Ian continues to look toward the mountains. His body looks relaxed, his eyes are squinting just a bit, and his jaw is cocked slightly to the left. I recognize this look; he did it a lot while sea kayaking in the Prince William Sound. He is thinking hard.

I get up to give him space. Grabbing my drink, I turn around to head back into the cook shack. The squirrels scurry for cover. "I'm going to go in for a while, get some food ready for us," I say. "I'll let you know when it's ready."

Ian nods and continues to sit deep in thought.

I walk into the shack and it's bathed in light. Also, good memories.

On the right is a picnic table. On the left is an open area in front of a wood-burning stove. A single-person bunk for the cook is next to the fireplace, and above that bed is a bookshelf stocked with *National Geographics* and random Tom Clancy–type books that have been left behind by hunters for decades. On the chair by the wall lies a copy of Jack Kerouac's *On the Road*. I smile and walk over.

When I open it, there's my name written inside. "Oh the things you have taught me," I say out loud. I shake my head in disbelief as I quietly laugh at the thought of what this book helped give me the courage to do.

When I came home after a few adventures, I found work as a substitute teacher in my hometown. I was well received as a substitute both by the teachers and the kids, mostly because I was known as a traveler and an "outdoorsman." It also helped that the local TV station owner and I created—mostly as a joke—a show called *Backyard with Mike Green*. This show was based on the premise of "getting outside and exploring the area within one gas tank from Hornell." It had the charm of watching a car wreck, with the allure of, "What is he going to say or do next?" Most people could not turn the channel. They had to watch. So the kids liked me, and in time I was prodded by loved ones to enroll in SUNY Brockport for a bachelor's degree in history and get my teaching certificate. It seemed reasonable to have this to fall back on, so I enrolled.

The fall before I graduated with my bachelor's and secondary education teaching certificate, I was asked to fill a position as a long-term substitute teacher for a tenth-grade global history class, for the remainder of the school year. I agreed.

All went well through the winter school season and into the spring. Then in early April the school's principal notified me I would have to stop teaching in mid-May if my New York Secondary Education Teaching Certification didn't arrive to the school district by then, because "only a certified teacher can teach to the state regent's test for tenth-grade global history."

I had mixed feelings about this. I like to follow things through. I don't like not finishing something that I started. But at the same time, I wasn't a fan of "teaching to the test" because learning about history is about your interpretation of the facts and how you internalize them. Learning about history shouldn't be about scoring high on a "one-size-fits-all test" to measure learning. Plus, I knew if I had to stop teaching in mid-May, I could get out to Alaska a whole month earlier. Which I was psyched for. These feelings came together in what I can only describe as an "out of body" experience in front of my fourth-period global history class while discussing the French Revolution.

I was standing in front of the class with my silver chalk holder in my right hand. As I turned to write the quote "Let them eat cake" on the blackboard, I quickly turned around and said out loud to myself, if not the students, "What the fuck am I doing? I used to be fun but now I'm teaching a quote about eating cake?"

As I spoke, it felt like I was looking down at myself and the classroom, as if I were a video camera high in the corner.

The students sat still in their chairs, mouths agape and eyes wide.

I continued, louder. "Man, I used to teach kids like you about life. But now I'm teaching you a quote about cake."

At this point I remember my out-of-body self looking down and thinking, *Where is this coming from?*

The students had begun to settle comfortably in their seats as I kept going. "From this point on, every Friday we will have a 'life lesson,' no matter where we are in the chapters. You all need to learn about what is going to help you in life, not just about eating fucking cake and Marie Antoinette."

At this the kids pushed back into their seats as if to keep from being part of this weird dialogue I was having with myself.

I wrote out on the board "Life Lesson Fridays" and began to feel a rush come over me. It felt like I was learning something, letting go of something, or maybe that I was shedding a skin I'd been trying to live in that didn't fit.

I was becoming a teacher, and for quite some time this hadn't been sitting well. And something about Marie Antoinette's phrase hit me. I was doing the safe thing, with a safe job, but it didn't feel connected to what I felt was essential and what I felt I was really good at: teaching people about life.

Something changed that day—both for me and the students. The life lessons were a huge hit. By the third week, my Friday attendance was 100 percent.

Then several weeks before I was scheduled to stop teaching so another "certified teacher" could come in to "teach to the test," I had another out-of-body experience. Again, it was with my fourth-period class on Friday. Maybe because they were my favorite class.

We were discussing the last week's lesson, titled "How Does the Media Influence Our Perception of Our Reality?" They'd been collecting newspapers (this was long before internet news) and identifying what percentage of stories were negative versus positive. And whether they were looking at a local paper or something from a bigger city, almost everyone found it was about 85 percent negative.

I pointed out that when you see that level of negativity, maybe it made us more fearful of the world, more fearful than we needed to be. And so I asked the kids, "If you had a flat tire on a road with limited traffic and a man you didn't know wanted to help you change the tire, what would you do?"

Before cell phones, the options were essentially to let him help, deal with it yourself, or wait for a trooper or someone you know to come along. And the class reflected the news: about 85 percent wouldn't trust him enough to let him help out.

There was an awkward silence as everyone digested this, and that's when my out-of-body experience got started. Again,

I began to see myself from the upper corner of the room as I spoke. I remember a sense of feeling free when I started talking.

"Guys, the lesson is that the news influences us and the choices we make," I said. "If 85 percent of the news is negative, we will see the world around us far more negatively than it really is, and if we go through life thinking everyone is out to get us, what kind of life is that? It takes courage to believe in the kindness of strangers. And to prove that you can, I will hitchhike from Hornell to Denali Park, Alaska, with no money or food."

As I said these words I was looking down at myself thinking, *What the hell did you just declare? You are going to do what?*

The kids were stuck dumb and I felt a heavy feeling come over me. I thought, *Oh shit. What have I started? Good thing I'm in good with the principal because I am going to need it.*

Then I came back to myself and started trying to do some damage control, saying things like, "OK, guys, as you know I've traveled a lot and I'm doing this because I have a lot of world experience. So I don't want you to think I'm saying that you should start hitchhiking. 'Cause I'm not."

At this point I knew I was rambling. I couldn't avoid the mess that was coming.

When the class ended, the kids left excited about what had transpired, and sure enough, I started to hear about it. By the end of the day, a couple teachers had come to see me. "What are you thinking telling kids that it's OK to hitchhike?" they asked.

"I didn't say that," I responded. "I said that it takes courage not to believe all the negative news and you can believe in the kindness of strangers."

That weekend the news spread, and beyond being told by the principal I'd better make sure the kids knew not to hitchhike, the comments overall centered on concern I'd end up dead in a ditch. Or raped and dead in a ditch.

My mother cried the first three times we discussed it. I told her that I had to do it, and she begged me not to right up until the end. But it didn't work.

The Monday after Mother's Day, I stepped out of my apartment freshly shaven, with neat haircut and clean clothes. My roommate's laughing comment from the day before echoed in my head as I put on my backpack: "You will not make it past Almond. You'll be home the same night."

As I lit a Fuente Opus X Double Corona—the finest cigar I could afford—I promised myself that I would make it, and on my legs, I headed west out of town.

I wasn't fifty yards from my door when a friend stopped me and offered me a ride.

Drawing off the cigar, I said, "No thanks. I'm going to enjoy this cigar and then start this adventure."

I smoked it to the very end. Then I slung my backpack off and found the sign one of my students had made for me. It fit inside a large ziplock bag, and read "WEST" on one side and "NORTH" on the other. It was simple, easy to read, and got the point across. Just like my route across North American. Go west and then eventually go north to Alaska. Pretty simple plan. As long as the driver was headed west or north I was headed in the right direction.

I was surprised how calm I felt. I knew I was about to start an epic journey, a Hero's Journey of my own. Hell, I'd done this road to Alaska before—a number of times. I knew there would be plenty of challenges in the 5,300 miles ahead that would demand a lot of courage. I also knew that between where I stood and Denali National Park I would experience kindness in response.

I was eager for the magnitude of the quest. It was for me, the people I would meet, and my students.

I'd also be smart. I'd use my sense of summing people up and decline a ride if I needed to.

My plan was simple. I wouldn't accept any money. In fact, I verbally stated out loud on the side of the road, "I will not touch money from now until I arrive in Alaska." I would accept food only after working for it, with the plan to only go into "family-owned restaurants" and ask to work for a sandwich or meal. I figured that being interested in or telling stories on a drive would also allow me to accept a meal or sandwich from a driver, if they offered.

Within my medium-sized backpack, I had a couple choice Grateful Dead shows to listen to, eight AA batteries, a dozen blank minidiscs and a small microphone on a wire to record both my conversations (with and without drivers knowing) and thoughts throughout the journey. I had a light two-man tent, sleeping bag, journal, water bottle, several sets of clothes, toiletries, rain gear, and soap. It was important to look and smell clean. If you feel clean you look clean. Plus I figured I'd get picked up faster. So I planned to bathe in the streams and rivers across North America.

Understanding I was giving up all control of my route, I sent resupply packages of batteries and minidiscs to two locations—Jackson Hole, Wyoming, and Whitefish, Montana. I had a "still barely friendly" ex-girlfriend in Jackson Hole and great friends north of Whitefish. So, I hoped to make stops there.

Happy with the sign and excited for the journey, I slung on my backpack, held the sign in my left hand, and thrust my right thumb out into the world. I said something that sounded near the Serenity Prayer, followed by a true Catholic-boy prayer finished off with, "Lord, don't let me end up in a ditch dead or raped then dead." And I was off.

At first, it seemed like a lot of cars slowed down to "take a look at me" but then kept going. I felt like a novelty. And maybe I was. I tried to remember when I'd last seen a hitchhiker let alone picked one up.

As I was scanning my memory, an old, rusty, blue Chevy Nova pulled over just ahead of me. My first ride.

As I opened the door, I immediately noticed the mangled fingers resting on the blue steering wheel. "Get in," a voice commanded.

The driver was a black-bearded man with a Vietnam vet baseball cap resting on his long, black, unwashed hair. His car smelled of cigarettes, and Pepsi cans littered the passenger foot area.

I blurted out, "Thank you. You're my first ride."

Embarrassed at seeming too excited and coming across as a rookie hitchhiker, I pulled the front seat forward and slid my backpack into the back seat. I sat down, shut the door, and introduced myself.

"My name's Mike Green," I said, with a little more cool.

I've since forgotten the man's name. However, I will never forget his story.

I instantly noticed his tight energy—it reminded me of when my friends and I would put a golf ball in a vice and cut off the white coating, which keeps the rubber bands from exploding in every direction. The driver reminded me of a white golf ball in a vice with a lot of his white coating cut away or worn away. But I felt safe.

As he got the car up to speed, he started talking, like so many other drivers would. They would simply look forward, hold the steering well as if it was a pillow on a therapist's couch, and bare their soul.

"I just came back from giving blood at the VA," he began. "If I don't give blood once a month, I get a headache. And when I get a headache I don't like people and that becomes a problem."

"OK," I said—thinking, this is going to be cool.

He continued. "I'm a Vietnam vet in case you didn't see my hat. I was a POW twice," he said in a quiet, matter-of-fact way. I noticed he was going only fifty-five miles per hour and didn't seem to be paying much attention to the cars on the two-lane road passing us.

"Wow," I said.

"First time they broke my fingers, wrists, and cut pieces of skin off my calves so it was hard to lie down. Have you ever tried to sleep without letting your calf muscles touch something?" he asked.

That was an easy one. "Nope," I said.

"Well I had enough of that shit and broke out. I hid from them for two days before a bunch of Americans came by. At first, I didn't say anything from where I was hiding. I didn't want to get shot. I knew they were Americans because they swore a lot. I eventually yelled out that I was an American and that Babe Ruth was a Yankee. When I said that I held my breath. The swearing stopped and I expected to hear bullets fly by my head. Then one guy yelled, 'Name a state,' and I called back, 'Texas!' Then he said, 'Everyone knows Texas. Tell me another.' I was pissed at this point and said, 'Fuck you, Texas sucks.' I started naming off a couple more states and then stopped and said, 'I've been a POW for too long to wait for you motherfuckers to ask me bullshit questions.' I figured if I used a lot of swear words they wouldn't shoot. 'I'm coming out. Don't shoot,' I said. I did and they saved me. It was just that simple."

Totally into the story, I breathed out, "That's incredible."

He chuckled as he turned left onto the on-ramp of Route 17 West. "And then Uncle Sam fixed me up and sent me back out there."

I drawled out a slow "Damn," as he got up to sixty miles per hour.

"I'm only going to the Belmont truck stop. I'll drop you off there. Maybe you can get a ride with a long-haul trucker or something."

"Fine by me. Yeah maybe."

He continued to look forward and rest his mangled fingers on the steering wheel. When he dropped me off at the truck stop, I got out and thanked him kindly.

As he drove away I just stood there, still, looking out at nothing in particular. I was stoned by the story I just heard.

Excited, I threw on my backpack and strode into the truck stop dining area and proudly proclaimed, "Who wants to be my second ride to Alaska?" People looked up, then turned back to their chicken fried steaks and coffee.

Immediately I felt like an idiot, with my sign and my bluster. What the hell was I thinking? From the response I got the sign might as well have said, "Dick."

I walked out dejected and mad at myself, but having learned a valuable lesson. Keep a humble profile.

I headed across the bridge and down the on-ramp.

As cars passed by, I would stick out my right thumb, hold my sign with my left, smile a genuine smile, and do my best to make eye contact as I continued to walk. This system seemed to work well. From that point on, whether outside a major city or on a desolate out-of-the-way road or highway, I never waited more than an hour for a ride.

My second ride was from a flatbed tow truck driver. He was headed only a short distance in my direction, but the small amount of time I spent with him was a gift. Like the first driver, he stared straight ahead and started talking.

He told me about his four-year-old daughter's journey since

being born. "One of the smallest preemie babies at that time." He told me of the ups and downs of his marriage, his daughter's health, and the health care bills. As his daughter got older, they could tell something was much different in her. She was extremely advanced with numbers, reading, and motor skills.

The driver swelled up with pride as he told me, "She was so advanced that doctors from around the world came to do studies about her. In time, those studies paid off our debt and my wife and I could breathe again. We're doing much better now, but hell, man, it was tough."

As my ride came to an end at the top of the Olean exit, I got out and thanked him, both for sharing the ride and his uplifting story.

"No, thank you," he said, as he double-clutched his rig into first gear. "Sometimes I forget how blessed my family and I are. And I'm remembering it now."

I closed the door and stepped down off the truck. A sense of wonder came over me. *And that was only my second ride*, I thought.

I headed down the on-ramp until I came to a spot with good visibility to both highway and on-ramp traffic. A driver stopped to pick me up, then another and another, until I eventually stood on the side of the road in Western Minnesota, looking at the wide expanse of horizon.

As I looked to my right and left, up the road and down, the realization of how epic this endeavor really was hit me. As I felt the weight of it, a heavy sense of dread hit me like the rushing turbulence of the passing semis. I was standing by myself on a lone highway, and all of a sudden I felt how much I was alone and truly in the middle of nowhere. Sure, I'd had good or even great rides so far, but nonetheless, my sense of adventure was falling away. *What the fuck am I doing out here?* I thought.

A symphony of negative talk swirled in my head. At the same time, car after car passed by without stopping, only adding to my dread. As I stood there with my sign out, I knew I had to get out of this funk and back to being with the adventure. I figured no one would pick me up if I looked this dejected. So as the cars kept whizzing by, I asked myself what I needed to get out of this. I began to self-coach. "Courage," I said out loud. "Courage to understand that there will be ups and downs on the road. Courage to overcome the emotional pitfalls. You got water and you ain't that hungry. Hell, you went three days without eating before. You can do it now if you have to."

The cars and semis kept passing, but now with each whoosh of air and tires I started to feel better. I began to look at each as an opportunity to try and connect with the driver, making it a point to try and look into their eyes. As I did this, I noticed more drivers tapping their brakes—as if to say, "Should I?" Still, no one stopped, but the drivers' hesitation showed some promise. Then I switched the sign to my left hand and began using my right to wave a simple hello. Not too strong like a Jeremiah Johnson wave of last desperate connection, but a laid-back raise of the hand you might get from a farmer driving his rig down a country road. Which replaced negative thoughts and feelings in my head and my body with the John Denver song "Take Me Home, Country Roads." Which left me feeling happy and welcoming.

After a while, another semi came barreling down the highway. I looked up to the driver closing in fast and gave him my farmer howdy wave—and he locked up the brakes. Fast enough to create smoke and skids and make the trailer bounce. "Damn," I said with a laugh. It worked. I began to "waddle run" toward the truck, my backpack bouncing to the left and right with each stride.

I stepped up to the semi and opened the door. The truck driver looked at me as if he was surprised that he'd stopped.

"Howdy," I said.

"Hello," he said back in an Eastern European accent.

Mistaking it for Russian, I eagerly attempted to thank him in what I thought was his native language. "Spasibo," I said.

When his half smile turned to a frown, I added quickly, "Sorry."

He replied proudly, "I am Polish. Get in."

I did and put my backpack between my knees. "I'm really sorry," I said again.

He smiled again as he ran through the gears getting up to sixty-five miles an hour. "No problem. You been in Russia?"

"Yes. But Poland is much prettier," I said.

"Where in Poland you been?" he asked.

As we headed west we talked about Poland's beauty. He told me that he planned to drive through the night, saying in his pretty-good English, "You can keep me not sleeping as I drive."

Which I did.

And for his part, he hauled ass in that truck, never even stopping at any weigh stations. He told me, "We stop when we no fuel."

I nodded my head in agreement and understanding, knowing it was going to be a long night. We told stories, asked each other questions, and from time to time looked over the map.

As the morning rose behind us, I let him know that Buffalo, Wyoming, would be a good stop for me. "From there I can make it over to Jackson Hole," I said.

"No problem," he replied.

When I got out of the truck I thanked him and wished him good luck. He did the same. As I crossed the highway and began to go down the meridian I noticed a woman wearing a backpack with a dog inside. Without thinking, I exclaimed, "What are you doing out here?"

She answered with some sarcasm. "Same as you but heading in the opposite direction."

Embarrassed but still excited to see my first solo woman hitchhiker ever, I replied, "Great! Where are you coming from and going to?"

"Seattle. Headed to Albany."

"Wow, I'm from Hornell, New York!" I was still excited. And she was still not impressed.

We chatted for about ten minutes about "being on the road." She was pleasant and intelligent, and we swapped a couple stories.

She told me she never waited more than ten minutes for a ride. "Must be because of the dog," she said. "People have a soft spot for a dog."

I told her I was headed to Alaska, which seemed to finally impress her, slightly. Then I added, "I'm sorry for asking such a stupid question earlier. I didn't expect to see another hitchhiker, especially one with a dog."

"No problem," she responded warmly. "I get it a lot." Wanting to get on with her day, she moved to part ways. "Never get dropped off on the front side or the first part of a town or you'll be walking your way all the way through it."

"Thanks," I said as I dropped my pack and began to feel for my cigar box. "I'm sorry I don't have much to give you but a cigar."

She smiled. "Thanks but I don't smoke cigars."

"No problem," I said, not to be denied. "Give it to someone that does. My life trajectory has changed for the better many times because of a fine cigar."

She laughed. "OK. I'll keep it and hope for the same."

As we walked up to the top of the meridian, I said "I'm thankful to have met you. I'm headed to Jackson Hole."

She said simply, "Me too."

We left each other crossing the eastbound lane.

"Be well," I said.

As I headed down the on-ramp toward the gas station, a car had already pulled over and picked her up heading east. Before getting in she waved back at me and I did the same, thinking that the courage to be on the road comes and goes, east and west.

I continued on until I eventually landed in front of a diner, which I noticed could use some clearing of cigarette butts and crushed beer cans that dotted the area.

I was hungry. Time to do some work for a meal. My first ask.

As I walked through the wide door, I set off a loud clanging of bells.

It was a typical western diner with a friendly atmosphere decorated with cowboys and steers pictures.

A kind and spunky-eyed lady in her sixties was behind the counter. Her apron noted her name. Hazel.

"What can I do for you, young man?" she asked.

"Good morning, Hazel. I'd like to speak with the manager or owner, please."

She took a breath and leaned back on her heels before speaking. "Oh. Well I'm in charge at the moment. What can I do you for?"

"Hazel, I noticed that your parking area and the bushes in the front could use some attention. I wonder if you would allow me to work for a simple sandwich?"

She again leaned back on her heels with an inhale of surprise. Her eyes darted around the diner to the customers.

"Oh, well we don't let people work that we don't know." She

seemed to be searching for what to say next. "Ah… we can just give you a sandwich and a cup of coffee to help you out."

The diner was quiet, and I was uncomfortable and strangely embarrassed. I hadn't figured it would be this hard.

I wanted to turn and leave, but I couldn't. I had to see this request through.

"I'm sorry but I can't accept that very kind offer. I have to work for my food. I'll just move on down the road. Sorry to bother you and these people in your diner. Have a good day."

Mouth agape, she spurted, "What do you need? For the parking area?"

"Simply a bag to put the trash in, Hazel," I said quietly.

The room seemed to lighten up and people went back to their eggs, coffee, and Reuben sandwiches.

Hazel instructed me where to put my backpack as she handed me a small trash bag.

Still feeling uneasy about asking to work for food, I headed out into the parking lot. As I picked up the tossed cigarette butts, potato chip bags, and random papers, I thought about the exchange. What made it so uncomfortable? As time passed, I came to realize that I'd been forced to dig for a kind of courage that was unfamiliar to me. The courage to ask for help in the form of a basic need. Food. And it wasn't easy. Although I didn't feel dehumanized for having to ask for a basic need, I could easily see how someone could. How that could eat away at self-esteem and bring someone to sink into a hole of despair.

I must have been deep in thought because the bag was almost full, and I kept going. Hazel had to come out to get me.

"Son, that's enough. Wow. I had no idea that all was out here."

Surveying the parking lot and bushes, I was astonished at

the improvement. "Yes, ma'am. I think picking it up made a difference."

Hazel held the door open and ushered me in with kindness. "Yes, looks much better. Now get in here, wash up, and eat."

I tied up the bag and did what I was told.

When I got back to the counter, Hazel motioned for me to sit near my backpack. A glass of water and an empty coffee cup were waiting for me.

Soon she disappeared and returned with a hamburger and fries, placing it in front of me with gentleness. "May God bless you and your journey," she solemnly said.

"Thank you, Hazel. I'm truly grateful for your kindness."

"Well, you worked hard out there. It can't be easy to pick up trash when you know everyone is watching. Most of the time people come in just asking for a handout. You didn't. Which is a new one for me."

"Yes, ma'am. It's new for me too. I never had to ask for food before." I said it in a matter-of-fact way between devouring fries.

Surprised and curious, she leaned in and quietly asked, "What's your story, son?"

"I'm hitchhiking to Alaska from New York."

"Alaska!" she exclaimed. "My dear, that's a haul." She instinctively grabbed the coffee pot and offered me some coffee.

"No, ma'am. Could I instead please have an iced tea with three lemons?"

She returned with my iced tea, shaking her head in amazement. "Does your mother know what you're doing?" she asked.

I laughed for many reasons "Yes, ma'am, she does. She cried three times trying to get me not to."

"Bless her heart," she said.

With my head between my two hands, I said, "Yes, ma'am."

It didn't take long for me to finish the meal, something Hazel noticed as well. Before I was about to leave, she came back with a full paper bag.

"You take this bag for when you get hungry again," she instructed me. "And call your mother."

Grateful but feeling uncomfortable, I took the bag and put it into the top of my backpack.

"Thank you again, Hazel, for your kindness."

"You're welcome. Good luck on your trip."

As I shouldered my backpack, I turned to say thank you again. Thankfully she was on to the next customer, coffeepot in hand.

Soon I made it to Jackson Hole, where a cowboy took me to my ex-girlfriend, Leighann, who unceremoniously handed me my resupply box and let me stay with her for a couple days. I met some interesting guys, pitched a tepee for Harrison Ford (true story), and kept making my way.

Then things got a little weirder.

Just south of Eureka, Montana, an old 1979 Thunderbird pulled up beside me and I jumped in the car. Inside was a guy who had a haircut like Elvis and the gaudy turquoise jewelry to match. His small frame sat close to the steering wheel and covered only half the driver's seat.

He said he was headed to an appointment in Eureka. "I'm going to get this prosthetic leg fitted better so when I get up into my truck it doesn't hurt my leg and create sores," he said.

We talked about this and that as he drove the large car around the bends. The Thunderbird rode smooth and easy, just like my grandfather's had, I noticed.

As we continued on, I noticed his right hand inching its way toward my leg. His having just had ulnar nerve placement surgery, as he'd told me, I gave him the benefit of the doubt. I thought maybe he just needed to stretch out his arm. But as we drove farther north his arm started traveling east up my leg. This created a firestorm of emotions in me.

First, I told myself to stay calm and in control. Second, I felt pissed that this was happening because I'd wanted to be able to tell my students back in New York that "I'd had no issues." And at this moment, I was having an "issue." Third, I needed to figure out how I was going to get out of this situation.

All these thoughts swam together in my head. I worked to stay calm and decided to say something powerful to show him I wasn't interested and that I wasn't going to be a victim.

"Ah… I see that your hand likes my leg," I said. As it was coming out, I thought, *What the fuck kind of comment is that?*

Immediately the driver turned his head from the road and looked at me. "Yes, I do," he said in a pleading voice. Followed by a full-on openhanded grab on my left leg.

The pleading tone of his voice coupled with his hopeful and lonely facial expression concerned me the most.

As this all went down I saw a road sign saying, "Eureka 7 miles, US/CA Border 14 miles." Again, in my head I was trying to keep calm. *Measure your response*, I told myself. *Don't piss him off but make it clear that you are not a victim.*

What came out was slightly different. "Well if you don't move your hand I will put a knife in your leg."

He didn't move or react at first. Then he slowly moved his hand away from my leg. After a pause he said, "I was just hoping that you go that way."

A pang of sadness for the guy came over me. Briefly. Still in reactionary mode I said, "Nope. I don't. But you are going to drive me through Eureka and drop me off without any problem."

His body seemed to get much smaller and frailer in the driver seat. He drove on at the same speed as before, looking straight ahead. He didn't fidget or stir. Neither did I. I didn't look at him or speak for a long time.

I spent that quiet time shifting back and forth trying to figure out where to place my anger. Was I pissed for having experienced this or was I pissed more because I would have to be honest with my students about the encounter? What would I tell them? How would I tell them?

The longer the silence went on, the more empathy I had for the driver. Still, I didn't let on. I just sat quietly and ready to strike out if he tried anything.

As we rounded the corner, the town of Eureka came into view.

"There is Eureka," he muttered.

"Yep. Can you please take me to the edge of town?"

"Sure," he said, as if nothing had happened or in a manner hoping to erase the earlier experience.

At the north edge of town, he pulled over to the side of the road. As I got out and started to shut the door, I turned to thank the driver for the ride. Without making eye contact he said, "You're welcome." He seemed to be even smaller than before. He was small, sad, and lonely. You could just tell.

Feeling sorry for him I quickly said, "I hope everything turns out alright for you."

He put his Thunderbird into gear and said, "Yeah. So do I."

The experience was over. I made it safe. I was not dead or raped. Or in a ditch.

I was alright. Pissed and emotional but OK.

I next found a ride with a local Thelma and Louise (actually named Rosebud and Sweetgrass; true story) who did their best to flirt and make my day a little better. Then an American and some Germans helped me get across the border to Canada—which is not always easy to do. From there, I made my way up toward the southwest side of Jasper National Park, an area that, in my opinion, has some of the most beautiful views in the world.

It was time to eat again. I found a small mom-and-pop restaurant on a lonely part of the two-lane road between a couple small towns. The restaurant was painted white and looked welcoming. But I noticed the gravel parking lot had cigarette butts peppered in.

I walked into the half-filled restaurant and everyone turned to look at me. I asked the woman behind the counter if I could speak with the owner or manager.

"I guess I'm the manager. We really don't have one," she said.

Nervous and uncomfortable for this part of the conversation, I said quietly, "Miss, my name is Mike Green. I was passing by your nice restaurant and noticed that you had some cigarette butts on the ground and some trash in those bushes. If you give me a trash bag I'll spend thirty minutes picking up your parking lot and cleaning out those bushes. All that I ask is for a sandwich in return."

Her eyes were kind. "No, that won't be necessary. I can give you a sandwich. No need to clean our parking lot."

"I'm sorry, miss," I said, looking her in the eyes. "I can't accept that. I have to work for my food. Do you have any recommendations where I could work for something to eat near here?"

She seemed puzzled at my answer. She shifted back and forth for a moment and then simply said, "Let me get you a bag."

Standing there feeling that everyone's eyes were still on me, I wanted to just walk out. Then an interesting question crossed my mind. I asked myself, *Why are you so meek when you ask to work for food? You should stand tall and just ask.*

I was deep in thought when she returned with a trash bag.

"Here you go," she said.

"Thank you, miss. May I please leave my bag inside?"

"Oh yes. Please do. Put it over there." She pointed to the corner booth.

I made a point to look at my watch as I put my bag down in the booth. As I walked out, I told myself to stand tall, knowing everyone was watching. And I did.

Outside, I thought on my experience of asking for food in exchange for work, and how I felt so meek when doing so. And why? As time passed and trash added to the weight of my bag, I came to the conclusion that courage comes in a number of forms, just like kindness does. There was the courage to step off the teaching track. The courage to trust in the kindness of others. The courage to follow through on what I'd said I would do, even after hearing all the negative comments about it and even when the journey felt overwhelming. And the courage to accept the acts of kindness coming my way, whether it was a ride or a meal.

I learned that standing in front of a perplexed stranger asking to work for food was hard. Doing so was taking another kind of courage. As I filled the bag, I realized I wanted to dig deeper and try to speak plainly without embarrassment going forward, as I asked for this basic need usually paid for by currency. I knew that these thoughts would continue to develop as my journey continued.

The woman came outside and called to me. "It's been over thirty minutes. Come on in and eat."

That night, I pitched my tent on a flat spot by the river that was just out of sight from the road. With clouds coming over the mountains, I'd decided to stop for the day and put up my tent before the weather came in.

I journaled that night until the rain came in and put me to sleep. My last thought was, *I hope it's not raining in the morning*. I hated taking down my tent in the rain just as much as I hated putting it up in the rain.

The next day, there it was. Rain. With a damp tent fly and cold river water on my face, teeth, and gums, a general dull feeling of adventure pulled me forward. Best as I could figure I was just over halfway to Alaska. And I knew the next four to five days would be through some of the most beautiful and desolate roads on the continent.

In the slight misty rain I got to the road. The majestic mountains were covered with gray clouds, and I was feeling morose. I decided to listen to some Grateful Dead on my MP3 player. As the song "Looks like Rain" played, the drops began to come down slightly harder.

I listened to Bob Weir plead and play as the cars passed by.

I will never forget that moment. As Bobby played on, I got more and more depressed and cold, thinking no one was going to want to pick up a wet hitchhiker. And then I heard the sound of a horn. A car had pulled over and I hadn't seen it!

I loped up to the car not wanting to seem too desperate. It was a Jeep Cherokee with a family inside. The father jumped out and opened up the back door. "It will be tight but we'll fit you in," he said.

I opened the back door and said thank you. In the back seat were two kids and the mother was up front.

"Thanks for picking me up," I said, doing my best to look at everyone in the car.

The mother said in an easygoing way without turning around, "No problem. We used to do it. Before kids." She laughed.

We drove on and made small talk. We discussed the area—"the only two routes to Alaska"—and hitchhiking. They were optimistic about my journey.

"We would have you over for lunch but we're headed to my mother's," the father said apologetically.

"No worries. It was good to get out of the rain," I said. Stating the obvious.

They dropped me off in front of a small restaurant, one known for great food, they said. The rain had finally stopped.

As I got out, I thanked them—and Mother Nature. Then they drove off.

I checked out the property. Like the others, it could use some work. Before I went in, I took a moment to center myself in a deeper courage. This time, I intended to ask with pride for the basic need of food. I walked in, and I did so.

The woman inside didn't hesitate. She said, "I've been wanting my husband to do just that." She handed me a bag, smiling.

I didn't feel awkwardness as I asked, when I worked, or when she called me inside to eat.

Again, a large spread of food was laid out before me—eggs, bacon, French toast, beans, and hash browns. It was a lot. I asked for tea instead of coffee between the usual banter I had come to expect and experience. She was impressed that I had "come so far and still had far to go."

Between bites, I wrote in my journal about the experience of the day and the rides that got me this far. I was happy, full, and warm.

The lady of the place came back with a to-go container.

"Can you fit this inside your bag, honey?" she said, with a grandma's aura around her soft eyes.

"Yes, ma'am. I will make it fit. Thank you very much. I'm grateful."

"Don't fret none. It's the least I could do. You made my day cleaning up outside." I could feel her good heart through her smile, and knew why this place was so popular. Her deep sense of caring made me feel, well, special.

I packed up and walked out.

A short distance away, a guy with a dog was walking back to his old-school seventies-era Ford truck. He called out, "Which way are you headed?"

"West and north. Trying to get to the Cassair highway up to the Alcan." I declared it as if I had my own ride.

"I can get you to Whitehorse," he said in an easygoing manner.

'Whitehorse!" I exclaimed. "That's like three days drive from here."

"Yep. I have a wedding in Whitehorse. Headed out now. Want a ride?" He did not seem fun, but he did seem trustworthy enough.

I put my gear in the back and we hit the road.

The driver was an electrician from Kamloops, Canada, and he drove his truck like he talked. Slow, deliberate, and in only four gears on the "tree." I realized real quick I was in for a very long ride when I saw he kept the truck always running under fifty-five. Also because he was a nice enough guy, but plain and boring. And he couldn't get his dog to listen to him, which drove me crazy.

As the next three days dragged on, I learned another form of courage. The courage to stick with my original declaration of "giving up all control" of the rides, distance, and time frames. Many times I thought of getting out at the next stop and calling it good. However, unless he kicked me out, I was stuck. Those three days through some of the most spectacular scenery in the world were difficult to the core. I grew with every rotation of the truck tire.

We parted ways near the north end of Whitehorse.

I was relieved. I had stuck to my word. I kept my cool and stayed in the truck, however painful it was.

A few more rides brought me to another small restaurant,

Fast Eddies, where I ate everything on my plate and enjoyed two trips to the salad bar. (I was incredibly hungry after having not eaten anything of substance for about three days.) The manager brought me a to-go bag of food for the next day, what would be my final day of hitchhiking. She wished me well and said I could pitch my tent out back. Which I did.

In the morning, I woke to wonderful weather. There was a light breeze with the strong scent of white spruce. Denali Park was within reach.

I packed up my gear and made it to the road, which was already busy with traffic.

The second car that passed me picked me up. The driver dropped me off on the south side of Fairbanks.

I was in great spirits. My goal was within three to four hours away.

As I stood on the side of the road, making eye contact with passing drivers with my thumb and sign out for all to see, the realization that I was going to make it came over me. The emotions were beginning to well up in me but then a car pulled over. I had to gain my composure.

The driver was headed to the other side of town and said he could drop me off near the Fred Meyer grocery store junction "where anyone headed out of town can get you close or to Denali." Good to his word, he did just that.

At midday I found myself on the right side of Fairbanks to get to Denali. I knew where I was after having driven this road many times.

I stepped off the side of the road to pull out the to-go bag and take in the moment and the views.

Satisfied and grateful, I sat down to enjoy the sandwich. While rooting around inside the bag I found a note that read, "I admire your courage. Keep well."

Waves of emotion came over me.

I sat there deep in thought and wonder, fighting back tears to eat my sandwich. I reasoned with myself. "I am not in Denali Park yet," I said out loud. "There's still a lot of ditch left between here and there."

But I was happy. I finished the sandwich in the hot sun, and even contemplated having a cigar but quickly decided it was a bad idea.

I stood up and shook off the soreness and emotions. My thumb took its position jutting out over the white line of the road while my sign found its spot thrust forward toward the oncoming traffic.

A bush veterinarian and his son picked me up and then dropped me off in Healy, leaving me within one ride of Denali Park's "Glitter Gulch." The locals call it that because all the hotels, restaurants, and shops cram together on a tight strip of private land on the east side of the Nenana River, with Denali Park across a bridge to the south. In the strip of hotels, restaurants, and shops was a place called the Smoke Shack. And this season I would be a bartender there and anything else they'd need.

In Healy, I found myself standing on the side of the road sobbing. Between the sobs I pondered my journey and how it was about to end. I was sad and happy. Laughing between the tears, I noticed a familiar van pulling over to give me a ride. It was my friend Big Mike.

Big Mike was at least six feet seven inches tall with a beard that was thick, long, and bushy. Only Big Mike's blue eyes and shockingly soft voice seemed to bring him down to everyone else's level.

"Hey, Beefcake," he said. (Another long, true story.) "What are you doing hitching?"

I wiped away the tears. "Ah man, I've got nine days of stories to tell you. I hitched up from New York."

Big Mike's eyes lit up like a blue moon. Wide, bright, and inquisitive. "What… Get in, man. Get in."

As we started driving, I sketched out some of the highlights of my adventure for him.

"Wow," Big Mike said. "Are you glad you made this whole journey?"

That was a big question I'd been sitting with a lot through the last weeks. I said simply, "Yes."

My journey across North America didn't start when I left my apartment. It started when I acknowledged I wasn't living up to my potential. That I had allowed others' ideas, plans, and need for security to determine my own path and experience.

I remembered the day I declared Friday our day for life lessons going forward. It was as if I was overtaken by something both familiar and unfamiliar. I would later read *The Artist's Journey* by Steven Pressfield, and he called what I experienced "listening to your muse." A muse lives or exists within your subconscious mind. It's your creative self. Your true self. That day my muse must have had enough of my fakery at being a teacher. It knew that my "classroom" was the world outside without walls, bells, teaching to the test, or attendance. It knew I was not showing up at my best. In fact, I was doing my best to fit my energy, hopes, dreams, and self into a mold that could never hold my existence. So my muse kick-started me into action to get out and live the life I was meant to live.

It started with the intent to teach my students what really mattered. And I soon taught myself. The journey called on my courage in ways that changed my life. The courage to go against the grain of common mindsets, outside ideas of the life you should be leading, and paradigms that "keep us safe." The courage to stick to my word when things got tough and no one was watching. The courage to hold my head high as I asked to work for food. The courage to pitch my tent in unfamiliar territory for a night of rest. The courage not to reveal all that was taking place inside me when the situation called for restraint.

I was learning that courage comes in many forms, yet threaded through each was the simple act of being aligned with your true self and true direction in life. Courage is a muse that serves your life's journey, allowing you to maintain integrity of path. To be true to who you can be and not settle for what everyone else thinks, feels, or wants you to do.

Something that I cannot explain happened that day in front of the students that echoed out with each step forward in my journey across North America, and echoed out through my life forever after. I opened into the courage to make a major shift from doing what I "thought I should and could" do for the rest of my working life. Heading out on this adventure was an act of courage that honored my true self. And from that, a lot of other courage emerged.

As we made our way through the final corner along the river leading into Glitter Gulch, I asked Big Mike to drop me off so I could walk the last stretch. Without a word he complied and pulled over the van.

Before reaching for the door handle, I looked out the cracked windshield. At the familiar business signs, tears welled up and I took a deep breath while Big Mike sat quietly. "Thank you for the ride," I said as my lips began to quiver.

I let the tears flow freely down my cheeks as I opened the van door to get my backpack. The action of sliding shut the door acted as a physical marker of this journey coming to an end, and I began sobbing almost uncontrollably. "See you around," I managed to say. Through my tears, I could see that Big Mike got it. "Yep, man. I will," he said.

I watched in silence as he drove away. After thirty-seven rides, after nine and a half days, I was finally here. Minutes from the familiar canyon of stores with their obnoxious signs all vying for your attention and money. I almost couldn't believe it.

My eyes still wet, I turned and started walking.

CHAPTER 3

Europe: Integrity

DINNER IS STEAKS on the grill, whole potatoes cooked in foil, and a fine bottle of wine paired with dried mango for dessert. Ian and I eat outside because it's majesty and we're rational men. We happily take it all in.

Off in the distance, the Parker squirrels keep on squeaking, while I notice Ian's eyes start to drift downward. His mouth opens, and I wish I had my camera. Instead I nudge him. "Eh, Englishman, we got chores to do."

"How do I have chores if I am the client?" he retorts, without opening his eyes or moving.

"Being a client has nothing to do with fetching water. There is work to be done. Let's get after it."

He and I spend the next half hour getting the rest of camp set up and then another hour fetching water. It's still light outside when we head up the steep stairs inside to the "bunk area."

The sound of our feet on the stairs, and even the angle of them, feel as familiar to me as an old friend's voice. At the top,

I turn around to walk toward my bunk. Ian's bunk sits across the loft.

The space is large and the light is sparse, with only four small windows. One of them overlooks the valley, a vast landscape of white spruce trees and distant mountains all around. I can still see the areas where the horses were tied out during last year's hunting season.

I point out the view to Ian, then I show him where I keep the med kit—under the bed just like I've always had it for years. "In case those bears get in," I say.

We're about ready for bed. We have a lot of hiking to do tomorrow, and I want us up early, and fresh. I figure we've got one more glass of scotch in us, to bring sweet dreams.

I pull out a bottle I keep in the med kit, the good stuff. As I dust it off and check the seal, Ian says, "Tell me about tomorrow."

"Well," I say, as I open the bottle. "It's not always the easiest part of the trip, physically or mentally. It's about when some clients wonder what they've gotten into—aside from the bigger challenge of dropping distractions and having to be with themselves. It'll just be us, pretty far away from any semblance of civilization or other humans. But you're going to swing it fine." I pour out two small glasses and hand him one. "And you'll see how the quiet feels even more powerful."

In a more serious tone I say, "As we hike tomorrow, I want you to think about what we discussed earlier. What is working? What's not working and what distractions are a part of that? And what are your truths, especially as they relate to being a father, husband, friend, and leader? What aren't you willing to do and what aren't you willing to lose?"

"Right, Mike… what's my map and what is my compass. Got it. Known and unknown." His voice becomes more serious. "And ultimately, my vision of my life going forward." Ian raises his glass and I do the same. It's a night of toasts. "I look forward to the chance to test my mettle."

Ten minutes later, we're each in our beds, in silence.

The notes of peat, honey, and heather are still on my tongue, and I take a minute to savor the taste before I close my eyes. Drinking this scotch tonight, before the challenge of the next days, feels especially appropriate. It's from the Highland region of Scotland around Loch Eil, near Fort William, where I spent an intense few months testing my own mettle, in ways I didn't expect.

It's where I discovered, and deepened into, the true meaning of integrity.

My mind takes me back.

In the summer of 2002, I found myself guiding four foster kids and their social worker, a woman from the Shasta County Foster Youth Rights organization, from Philadelphia to London, to Scotland and back again. My job was simple: get them all to their meetings in Scotland, about "the evolving rights of foster youth in a country where foster youth rights are very progressive," and get them home without incident. And I did.

The kids had a great time. They loved learning how to travel. I can't say the same for their social worker, who was miserable, always wore a scowl, and insisted on wearing heels wherever we went. But it was a quick, easy trip, and I enjoyed exploring the towns while everyone else attended their meetings.

One day, I was waiting at the Edinburgh train station. I had about thirty minutes before my group arrived and we'd take the direct train back to London. As I waited, I walked around, a hot cup of tea in my hand, with the intention to find some gum that would deaden the smell of Guinness on my breath.

In those thirty minutes, a very important moment in my

travel history took place. High up the rack of magazines, I spied a picture of a man clad in fur, with a regal golden eagle on his right arm. He was sitting on top of what looked like a sturdy horse—or was it a pony? Either way, the sky behind him was a marvelous blue. In stark contrast to the picture was the magazine title: *Wanderlust*. I bought it immediately, knowing full well I would wait to read it when I could focus. I also knew that I would meet this man one day and find out what it took to live like that. (And sure enough, four years later I would. But that is another story. Thankfully one also in this book.)

I went to collect my group, boarded the train, and decided to sit with them—at least until our tickets were punched. The kids, being kids, smelled the Guinness right away. But I didn't care. In less than twenty-four hours we'd be on our plane back to the States.

After I saw them to Philly, I headed up to Rochester, New York, for a visit with my friends and family.

Just like usual, they all asked me, "Where have you been this time, Mike?"

As soon as I responded that I'd just returned from Scotland, the next question—without fail, and mainly because of the movie *Braveheart*—was always, "Did you get to the Highlands?"

I would then answer, "Nope, just the south." Or if I wanted to impress them, I would say, "Just the Lowlands." If the conversation progressed further I would ultimately feel as if I failed. A pretty deep feeling of failure, actually.

This feeling wasn't something I experienced often in my life, and I didn't like it. And as the days and conversations continued, I became downright embarrassed I hadn't gotten to the Highlands.

I was having a conversation about this with Bill Castle, a man I admired a great deal as a fellow traveler, when he stroked his long, wise, white beard and said, "Well, why don't you just go back and be a lumberjack?"

Later that night, after four or five Guinesses, I decided I would.

I'd first head to Alaska for the fall hunting season as planned, to work as a wrangler for a big-game hunting outfitter named Coke Wallace. Then I'd head back to Hornell for Thanksgiving, make some more money cutting down trees and grinding stumps with a great local man, Jim Hess, whom I'd worked with since I was fourteen. Then I'd go.

All went according to plan. I arrived in Great Britain mid-December

Heading from the "Lowlands" into the "Highlands" is distinctly rich to the eyes. The small rolling hills morph into steep, tall mountains surrounding lakes, or "lochs." Small roads twist and turn through small hamlets called "kiln" or "Glencoe." The region is small on population but huge on spectacular views, with or without rain.

I made my way to the local Outward Bound School where I spent the remaining weeks before the Christmas holiday. After accompanying some of the instructors into the Cairngorms for a cold, foggy, and damp two-day orienteering trip—"perfect orienteering weather, can't see 'fuk awl'"—I moved on.

I next found a hostel in Fort William run by a crazy, but helpful, woman. When I told her my plan, she handed me the yellow pages and instructed me, "Look under forestry. You will not find it under 'lumberjack,' that is for sure." She said this with a roundhouse laugh as her eyes were rolling in the back of her head.

I took the phone book with a bit of hesitation and looked

under forestry. There it was. Fergus Shaw Forestry. She looked at the number, dialed if for me, and waited with the anticipation of being about to listen to something good.

Standing in front of this strange woman, I waited as the phone rang.

A man on the other side answered calmly. "Fergus Shaw Forestry." I was surprised at how easily I understood him—normally I had to really concentrate to understand the Scottish brogue.

"Yes, sir, my name is Mike Green and I want to be a lumberjack."

Silence.

Then an exclamation in full brogue. "A lumberjack!"

Me being me, I acted as if everyone knew and understood what a lumberjack is. "Yeah, a lumberjack. You know, someone who cuts down trees."

Silence again. This time he answered with bewilderment. "Are you fucking putting me on, man?"

"No. I want to be a lumberjack. You know, use chain saws to fell trees." I emphasized the word "fell," so he'd know I knew something about cutting down trees.

There was a long pause. I could feel he was winding up a doozy of an answer.

"We don't have any lumberjacks in Scotland!" he said.

Not to be deterred, I said, "Oh. Well I can run chain saws, stump grinders, and bucket trucks." All true.

"For fuck's sake, man, are you putting me on?" I could tell by his intensifying tone, brogue, and cadence that he was getting impatient, and that I had only a couple more chances to convey my desire to work in "forestry."

"No, no, no. I'm here in Fort William, and I want to work in forestry cutting down trees, you know, with a chain saw."

This slowed our conversation down to a normal level. "Oh… so you want to be a feller? Why didn't you just say so?" he said.

"Yes, yes, a feller." Then he started dealing out the next couple of questions as if he was casually dealing cards. "Or do you want to be a brasher?"

A brasher is the one who cuts all the limbs from the ground up to about five feet so that a machine can come in and grab, saw, and process the tree in a matter of thirty seconds. But I had no idea of this at the time. So of course I just said, "Yes, a brasher," as if I were ordering something off the menu.

"Or do you want to be a cut to waste man?" This job I later learned is a man who just walks up and down the hillside cutting all the limbs and remaining trees to a length of less than three feet so they'll decompose quicker.

Still not willing to show my hand that this was the first I'd heard of such jobs, I said, "Yep."

Then he threw in a joker of a question by asking me, "Do you want to run the sky winch?"

Intrigued, full of confidence, and still not to be deterred, I said, "Yes, a sky winch."

I could tell he was running out of terms by his breathing. He was calming down and I was starting to have hope he'd give me a shot.

"What about being a chokerman? I need one at the start of the year."

I panicked at the mention of the new year—my money was running out and I needed work soon—but I plunged ahead. "Yes, yes, chokerman, I've done that on skid steers." Which was a half-truth at least.

I thought quick as I looked at the hostel manager. She was delighted at the comedy of my way of interacting with this complete stranger on the phone. Plainly stated, I am goofy.

Not to lose my chance I said to him in an earnest, honest, matter-of-fact way, "How about I hitchhike down to you and we can talk this over face to face?"

Another exclamation from him. "Hitchhike? Are you off your fuckin' head, man?"

Calmly, I returned the volley. "Ah, that's nothing. I hitchhiked up from London. Not to worry. I will see you in about two hours." (I gave myself extra time here. You never want to be in a rush when hitching. It's a rule of the road—it sends off the wrong vibe.)

"But it's piss down raining, man."

I simply said, "Not to worry. See you in two hours." And with that, I confirmed his address and insisted I would come, even after he wearily stated he would come to Fort William to meet me. I figured if I hitched all the way down he would see that I was serious. Besides, I wanted him to see that I wasn't afraid of any "piss down rain."

After writing down the address, I turned and looked out the window. Fergus was right. It was pissing down rain.

The interesting thing about hitchhiking in the rain is that the harder the rain comes down, the quicker you get a ride. I made it to Fergus fast.

It was a big shop with tools, trucks, and heavy equipment everywhere, and it smelled like axle grease and heavy hard work. Fergus was working on putting back together a chain saw when I walked in, his hands shaking as if he was four days from his last drink. I did my best not to act like I noticed. Besides, he didn't seem to care.

He stood there in the single-bulb light looking at me with part disbelief and part admiration. I knew this because he later told me so.

We talked about my journey, the terms of my work, when

I would start, and the type of men I would work with. The ladder seemed to be very important. In fact, it was the most important point of our "business discussion." I was struck dumb with the change in him as we talked about it, as if he was telling me a deep secret or that he was a direct descendant of William Wallace himself. (Something I was told twice by two others on this Highlands adventure.)

Another serious point to be made: my soccer loyalties. "If those fuckers who are picking you up ask you if you are a Rangers or Celtic fan," he said, "for fuck's sake and all that is holy, say Celtic, man. Celtic! If you don't, they will leave you far away from anywhere and never work with yous again."

At the time, I didn't understand the deep religious divide at play in what he said, but I went with it. "Right. Celtic. I am a fucking Celtic man all the way," I said.

Fergus laughed and offered me a hot cup of tea. We got on well, and I had the job. But I still needed to find work for three weeks to make it to my first paycheck.

So, I did what I thought made sense—hitchhiked to the northwest up toward the big estates, with their associated house, barns, maintenance sheds, sheep, and lots of fence—all of which needed maintaining. After passing an estate or two, I found a large house to the left slightly down the hill. It was freshly painted and long, with toys scattered around. As I walked up to the door, I could hear kids running around and a baby crying.

"Well, I'm here," I told myself. "Let's do this." And with that I knocked.

The door opened to a pretty woman holding a toddler. Another baby in a bassinet was crying in the background.

It was obvious she had her hands full, and she and I had a genuine moment without words. I looked at her, she looked at me, and I looked to the baby in the bassinet. "Would you like me to pick him up?" I asked in a gentle manner.

She hesitated slightly and then said, "Yes, please. Come in."

As I came into the house, two girls ran over, talking and showing me their toys, as the mother, Elsbeth, and I did our best to hold a conversation while I held the now-quiet baby.

I stated my case and mission, plainly and without a hint of begging. She said, "Oh, my husband and I traveled around Australia working."

Over time we had tea, the baby slept in my arms, and the girls lost interest in me after having showed me all their toys. Soon, the door opened and the father walked in. A flash of panic hit me at the optics of the picture he was about to witness. Me, a complete stranger, holding his little boy at the table with his wife.

I stood up slowly and said hello. Elsbeth told him what brought me to their home, and he welcomed me kindly.

His name was Paulo. He was an Italian Scotsman whose father came from Italy to Scotland to work. He looked Italian but he spoke and swore like a Scotsman.

Paulo and Elsbeth became great friends. They gave me work, food, and even a car to drive, in return for "doing all the things that I don't want to do," Paulo said. This included picking rocks out of the fields, mending and taking down fence, and most importantly, keeping "the fuckin' dim sheep from dying in the downed fence." I answered that I would do my best. Which I did.

And then it was time for me to begin the work that brought me back to Scotland.

I stood out front of the hostel on a cold and still morning, waiting for my new coworkers to pick me up. Thick frost laid heavy on the nearby branches and burning coal from nearby chimneys hung in the air in a black sort of fog.

My Filson oilskin pants and jacket were so stiff from standing outside for so long without really moving that I had to take my coat off to get into the car.

A man named Angus was driving. He looked young but yet old, in the way of someone who has consistently made bad decisions in life. Tom in the back seat was older. They spoke so quickly and with such thick Gaelic accents I could barely understand them.

After the cold pleasantries had passed, they said, "Why the fuck are you wanting to work in forestry?"

I hesitated before I answered because I knew my answer would be the foundation of our relationship. "I've traveled around the world doing jobs I was curious about. For example, I wanted to know what it was like to be a commercial lobsterman, so I worked as one for over a year in the Gulf of Maine." I hoped this would set the tone that I was a badass hard worker. And it seemed to, or at least make them curious—while waiting for the ferry, they asked a lot of questions about where I'd traveled and what work I'd done.

All the while, Angus continued driving like a Formula One driver through the one-lane roads, and eventually we made it to the work site.

A big burnt-orange piece of equipment like I'd never seen before was parked on the road. There was a small cab for the driver in front and another cab was offset farther back, with a thick, long, moveable tower with pulleys and cables at the "at ease" position. Huge, wide balloon tires stuck out past the fenders. I learned this piece of equipment was the sky winch.

It was parked near an impressive thirty-five-foot-tall stack of cut trees. The tops of the trees pointed up the steep hill, and the cut ends pointed down.

The razed hill wasn't a pleasant sight. I would later come

to look differently at the stumps and stacked trees, but when I first saw it, I felt depressed. I wasn't entirely sure if it was all because of the cut trees or if other things were starting to weigh on me, too. Was it in part because Angus drove like a maniac, cussed every other word (that I could understand), or because I now smelled like roll-your-own cigarettes? Or was it because the hill was so steep? Or because the rain had started and my Filson pants, warmed in the car, were now getting stuck on my cold legs? Or maybe it was because I was realizing for the first time, *Man, this is going suck.*

I followed Angus like a lost dog as he went to check the fluids on the sky winch and turn on the power. I did my best to understand him and act like I understood all he was saying. At the same time, Tom was setting up a stove to make tea.

Angus moved into the front cab and said—or at least I thought he said—"I hope you are good luck and this bitch starts." It did. "Fucking hell, this bitch is bad arse," he added with a smile that made me want to brush my teeth.

"Great," I said, and moved out of his way. The smell of diesel fumes filled the air.

Angus barked at me from behind the sky winch, something I interpreted as wanting me to walk ahead of him and make sure nothing would puncture the tires. I signaled OK, and walked forward as Angus revved up the engine and released the clutch.

The sky winch lurched forward with confidence. Angus, looking like someone right out of a Mad Max movie, was grinning, a cigarette wedged between his lips and one eye closed.

In time Angus stopped the sky winch and climbed down to the tower. He first looked at the hill of neatly downed trees, then with his hands on his hips he jumped back into the front cab and moved the sky winch about ten feet forward. Again, he jumped out of the front cab, deftly made his way to the base of the tower, looked up the hill, and smiled. He yelled something to me, and I signaled something positive back. He then turned around, looked downhill, stuck out his right arm as if to measure ninety degrees from the base of the sky winch tower. As he did this his rain jacket fluttered this way and that way. He didn't seem to care—his body language implied he was satisfied and proud of himself. He jumped back in the front cab, set the brake, and let it idle.

"I got her right where she needs to be," he said as he climbed off the winch. "Centered up the hill and with great stumps behind us to secure the tower." He was happy, and manic. "Cup of tea for us as this bitch warms up." With that he strutted toward Tom and the steaming teapot.

Angus and Tom talked over a plan as we drank our tea in the rain, almost as if I was not there. I looked in the direction they were pointing, nodded, and grunted occasionally, too. The hot tea was nice and comforting. However, I knew if I didn't start moving I would be getting cold quick. And in the thick, damp cold, it would be hard to get fully warm again. Especially when it was so early in the day.

We finished our tea and they both climbed on the sky winch to run the hydraulics to raise the tower. My job was to provide tension on the cables and keep them away from the winch and from getting caught on anything. Walking backward pulling the cables provided the movement I needed to get warm again.

Angus called out, "Take this rope, pulley, and cable to the top, find a strong tree, set it up, and come down. Don't get the fuckin' rope tangled in the trees." The rope that wasn't supposed to get tangled was on a large spool, which Angus would run as we advanced up and down the steep hill.

Tom was patient. He told me, "The trick of this job is to stay on top of the down trees. If you don't it's a fuckin' headache."

"Right," I said, as if I knew enough to agree.

I slung the heavy cable and pulley over my shoulder as if I were in a cigarette commercial. This was a mistake—the impact nearly knocked me over. Thankfully, Tom didn't notice. He was too busy holding the rope and beginning the task of "staying on top of the trees."

We started off cold and wet. Soon, we were huffing for air and wet. It was hard and frustrating work that required focus and squirrel-like balance. Trying not to fall down between the wet branches, while carrying a heavy cable and pulley up a steep hill, while not getting the rope tangled in the branches. Falling between the tree limbs would cause you to fall about three feet down to the ground. Which meant you would then have to climb back, on top of the fallen trees, up a steep incline. And I knew I could break a limb if I fell with my leg stuck in the branches.

Making it to the top of the hill took longer than I expected, was harder than I wanted it to be, and was a stark realization of how hard this job was. Tom was pleasant, measured, and encouraging throughout the experience, though, which made me like him.

Having reached the top before me, Tom tied the rope around a nearby tree, looked downhill, turned around again, and started climbing a large, thick tree. As he climbed, he cut the downhill branches off with a sharp handsaw. When he'd made it about fourteen feet up the tree, he called down and instructed me to bring up the cable with the pulley.

The pulley had the circumference of a large dinner plate, which made it difficult to climb up without it getting caught on branches. Carefully, I climbed within arm's reach of Tom and he used the cable to "choke the tree" with the pulley facing downhill. Meaning he looped the cable around the tree and pulled the pulley through the loop to create a choking effect.

Satisfied, he nodded and told me to go get the rope and not let it get tangled in the branches. This seemed like a theme for the day. I climbed down as efficiently as possible while Tom rolled a cigarette and looked out over the landscape. I grabbed the rope and hurriedly climbed the tree with the rope in my hand, careful not to get it tangled. Satisfied that I'd done well, I looked in the same direction as Tom.

The clouds had lifted somewhere in the struggle up the hill, and below us I saw a quilt of powdered-sugar-white hills, finger-shaped dark blue bodies of water, and a patchwork of green forests.

I remarked it was a beautiful sight.

Tom took the rope, threaded it through the pulley, and handed it to me as he kept the dying cigarette between his lips. "It's a keen area," he said with a nod, as he motioned me down. "Hold the rope tight."

We pulled enough slack through the pulley to get us started down the hill. Going up was dangerous enough but now we had the forward momentum to worry about, too. Just thinking of getting a foot, ankle, or leg stuck between the limbs brought a sense of dread.

I focused on foot placement as Tom took the rope. We eventually made our way to the sky winch, where Angus unceremoniously took the rope from Tom and quickly threaded the rope into a wire rope "catch" that used the force of the pull on the rope to grip or bite the thick cable. In time the rope pulled the cable up the hill, through the pulley, and back to the sky line. With that step complete, Angus and Tom were visibly satisfied.

With yet another cigarette between his lips, Tom leaned in to make sure I could hear him over the engine and the moving cable. "We're only half done with the setup," he said.

"What's next?" I said.

"Tea," Angus spit out. "Tea is what is next!" He jumped down and walked to the flat spot where the kettle was on a propane stove.

As we stood around waiting for the pot to boil, Angus pointed his dirty leather glove toward the back of the sky line. "See how those two cables attach to the tower at ninety-degree angles?"

Yes," I said. "So that you have support both forward and side to side, right?"

Angus nodded toward the sky winch as he did his best to keep his cigarette between his lips. "When we're done with tea, we will tighten them up a bit. Then we will attach the beast of a carriage and attach the cable to it. It can be a bitch of a job."

I just nodded like I knew what he was talking about. Mainly wanting to assure him I was picking up what he was laying down.

With tea finished we went about the second half of the setup job, and it was just as much of a slog.

With the main cable taut, the carriage waiting, and the winch ready to go, Tom turned to me. He pointed to the main cable. "Don't ever stand underneath that cable," he said. I nodded again in appreciation of his pointing this out. "I'm going to show you how this all works," he continued. "Stay close to me, and always have a plan to run away from cables, chains, and trees moving down the slope. It's best to have a hole to jump into."

As I was internalizing his ominous directions, I started looking around for my planned route or hole to jump into.

"Listen to the commands I give Angus. Stop, haul back, and haul in are the basics. Any questions?"

Blankly, I said, "Nope."

With that Tom spoke into the radio, "We're ready." Instantaneously, the sky winch roared and pitched a black cloud. The carriage passed us with a whorl, then stopped, changed directions, and spitted out the chains and heavy iron ring. There was momentary silence and then the distinct sound of chains falling into a pile.

Tom sprang into action, grabbing the chains just under the iron ring with one hand and picking up the rest with the other, as if he was a circus performer holding a large snake. Or maybe more accurately, an enormous squirrel bounding about with a mighty python.

He quickly scampered toward the cut ends of several trees and I followed behind as best I could.

"You need to choke as many trees together as possible for each haul, to stay efficient and so Angus doesn't get mad," he said. "Also, the more trees you choke the more space you have to work. To choke a tree, go to the cut end, wrap the chain around it twice, hook it to the release button at the end of the chain, and do the same with the other set of chains. Watch me."

The task completed, arms cut up from the battle, Tom said, "Come with me. I'll show you where to stand before you give Angus the command to haul in." Stopping midstride, he turned to me and looked me right in the eye. "Never give the command when you are on the downhill side of the load. And never give any command until you have a clear escape route in case fuck all happens."

"Thank you," I said, as if he just said something that would save my life. Which I'd later learn more times than I wanted to experience was the truth.

Satisfied with our spot, Tom spoke into the radio. "Haul in," he said.

The sky winch roared and soon the ends of felled trees rose up into the air, slowly at first and then in a flash, leaving their tops dragging across the ground until Angus stopped the carriage and pulled the lever to drop the trees to the ground.

Tom gave a grunt and a nod and started to look for the next batch of trees to choke as the carriage made its way up the steep hill. Eying the carriage calmly, he commanded, "Stop."

The heavy chains fell with great force to the ground. He grabbed them and the iron ring, and started toward several cut ends of trees. Then he stopped.

"See how there's not enough length of cable and chains to choke those trees?" he asked.

"Yes."

"Now I'm going to teach you how to get more slack. Watch me." He made a quick wrap of the chains around a stump, then gave the command to haul back. As the carriage slowly went uphill, it pulled out more cable. "Stop," he commanded. Then the carriage slowly came back downhill and stopped where it had started. Tom now had more than enough slack to reach and choke several large trees together.

Impressed, I said, "Pretty slick."

"You got to know how to work the carriage, cable, and chains or you won't last out here. It's grueling work already. No bother to make it harder."

Nodding, I moved to an area I believed to be a safe place before he radioed to haul in.

I was wrong. Another teachable moment for Tom. "What's wrong with where you are?" he asked.

Looking around, I noticed I could get hit with the tops of the trees as they headed down the slope. I stated this and Tom nodded. He pointed up the slope and said, "I always give myself ten meters more that I think I need. This rule has saved me plenty of times."

Half kidding, I said, "What if I don't know how long a meter is?"

Tom stopped and thought. Then he quipped, "Fuckin' Yank. Haul in." With that, the trees tore off the mountain.

The next couple of loads Tom taught me more tricks of being a chokerman that balanced both safety and keeping Angus happy. "Don't send a small load down to Angus or you will hear about it," Tom said. "Do your best to keep the loads full and everything will go better for you, the equipment, and especially Angus's temper. If he gets off his head…" He sighed. "Just remember you have to ride back with him."

We did a couple more loads before Angus declared it was time for lunch.

We ate in the rain, mostly in silence, looking up the hill.

To our left was a sweep of felled trees that reminded me of spread peacock feathers, without the vibrancy. To the right was a helter-skelter wasteland of stumps and small or dead trees. At the bottom of the hill was a surprisingly neat pile of trees choked from the side of the steep slope—ghostly white and gray reminders of what once was.

We finished our lunch.

Tom announced that I would now run the chains for the first time and he would call in the commands I relayed to him.

In time, the sky winch roared to life and up came the carriage.

I forgot to say "stop" and Tom had to call it out without my prompting. That was my first mistake. "Sorry," I said. "It won't happen again."

"You got this?" Tom asked.

"Yep. I'm ready."

When the choker chains came crashing down to the ground, I leapt into action. Wanting to make up for the missed call, I grabbed the chains under the large iron ring and swung them over my shoulder in a quick, powerful manner. The large iron ring landed on my back with a thud and almost knocked the wind out of me. This was my second mistake.

Tom was gracious enough to show me what trees he wanted to be hauled next. I did my best slinging the chains around the three thick trees hooking up the quick release. I stood there looking at Tom for a sign of confirmation.

Standing uphill on a felled tree, Tom just looked at me. He shrugged his shoulders and called out, "You can't be on that side of trees when you haul in."

"Oh right. I was waiting for you to tell me that I choked the trees right," I said, surprised at his tone.

"I'll let you know when something isn't right," he said flatly.

"Ok, then," I retorted. "Haul in."

"Haul in," Tom commanded into the radio.

The trees began their mournful rise toward the carriage, followed by a jerk downhill into the neat pile. As they moved, Tom offered commentary on my first haul.

"You'll have to be quicker to call the commands to stop the carriage. Angus is off his head most days. If you fuck up, you'll hear about it from him. And not through the radio. You'll be able to hear him from all the way up the slope. If you are going to take your time, take it when you choke the trees. If the haul's a good one, Angus will be happy. If you take too much time and the haul is small, you will hear about it," he said. "Never call 'haul in' from the downhill side of the choked trees. And most importantly, if you hear a snap, pop, or bang, get down. That's the sound of a cable snapping and if it hits you, it will kill you instantly. Don't forget to have an escape route too."

I listened and thanked Tom for the direction. Then I called stop, leapt into action, grabbed the chains, and choked another haul of trees. I again moved up to where Tom was standing and called, "Haul in." The haul did its thing and Tom said, "Good. What trees are next?"

I pointed to two large ones.

"Good choice, but are any other trees on top of them?" he asked.

When I nodded, he pointed with his free hand finger (the other now had a lit cigarette, which I took as a good sign, of reasonable trust) to two others. "That one and that one. Then you can have a clear choke of those big ones."

"Got it," I said, then added, "Stop."

"This next haul I want you to practice 'haul back' by wrapping the chains around a stump," Tom said.

"OK, no problem," I said.

When the carriage was just past us, I called, "Stop." When it did, I grabbed the chains, pulled a bit on the cable, found a good stump, and wrapped the chains around it. With Tom looking on, I called, "Haul back."

I held on to the ends of the tightening chains and called out, "Stop." When the carriage stopped, I released the chains and moved forward, slipping on a wet log and nailing my shin. I did my best to act as if it didn't hurt that bad. Tom noticed anyway and asked, "Are you alright?"

"Yes. Fuck, that hurt."

"You'll either get better shoes, learn more where to step, or buy some shin guards. I suggest you get better at stepping and in the meantime get some shin guards at the sports shop," Tom said with a smirk.

"Noted," I replied as I hugged the choke chains around a tree.

The afternoon labored on, with the mist turning to rain and rain turning back to mist several times through the day. We took a break for tea and then continued to work until 3:30 p.m. Then Tom said, "Time to go. We need to meet the ferry at 4:10."

I did not protest as we headed down the slope.

We met the ferry without incident and had an uneventful car ride back. I did my best not to fall asleep.

As I stepped out of the car in front of my hostel, I could tell that I was already getting sore.

Undressing in my room, I made a mental list of things I would need to purchase to make the next day more tolerable. Shin guards, a teacup, and another set of gloves for the afternoon. I took a shower and took inventory of the black and blue marks on my quads and shins. I also could not help but feel the burning feeling you get in fresh wounds on my wrists and forearms. And I felt worse than the banged-up shins, quads, and cuts revealed. I knew I only had a short time to get to the store and if I stopped moving around, I would stiffen up.

The sports shop was closed for the night so I made a note to return the next day. Then I made my way to a hardware store and bought gloves. Next I stopped off at a food store for a large travel mug and groceries. Pasta, sauce, and vegetables. I also picked up a small hand broom I could use to brush off my Filson oilskin pants. They were rugged and great to have on my first day, but they also soaked up dirt, sawdust, and tree sap. To be respectful to Angus and his car, I would use the broom to brush off the ruminates of the day's work. I was proud of my unplanned purchase.

Yet my mood as I walked back to my hostel was melancholy and pensive. "What am I doing here?" I asked myself, aware it was only going to get harder from here. "Do I really want to work this job?" All this swam in my head as I made and ate my dinner.

The next day I waited in the cold, wet street to be picked up by Angus and Tom, coal soot again heavy in the air. It seemed it was always just below the low clouds creating a layer of black gray that sat underneath lighter gray under white clouds. The dark blue water of Lock Eil that I could see made the cold feel colder, or was it the heavy gray all around? Either way, I was not in an excited mood. As I waited, I wondered what the day would bring.

It began similarly to the day before, with extreme driving coupled with swearing, and the wait for the ferry. Before we got started, Angus growled between sips of tea, "You are gonna have to pick it up today. Hauls are gonna have to be quicker."

I nodded, slung the rest of my tea on the ground, and headed up the slope. At his words, something inside me moved. It was as if my value of working hard was being questioned.

The day continued with Tom calling in commands while teaching me, and Angus running the winch. Grueling work done against a backdrop of smoke and light conversation. Our goal was to finish the slope in time to "piss off early for the Celtic and Ranger match" that evening.

We worked throughout the morning at a hard pace, and I did a good job choking. My morning soreness had worked its way out of me, making way for soreness later, I was sure. My shins got hammered a couple of times and I could tell they were bleeding underneath my pants.

We finished the afternoon with a lot done. As we came down the hill, I saw the large pile of trees differently than I had the day before. I looked at them as an accomplishment.

We headed to the pub as planned.

The remainder of the evening and through the match, I was the runner for the pints (perfect artisan pours of Guinness that I deeply appreciated). I didn't mind. They picked me up for work, Tom kept me safe, and Angus did his best to teach me about "the fuckin' winch." I saw it as paying it forward.

The Celtic fans were wild and loved to sing songs about the oppressive English, the greatness of Scotland, and the glory of the

Celtic team and history. In between the songs were wonderfully creatively ways of showing disgust of the Ranger players, fans, and anyone else that did not like Celtic.

Celtic won 2–1 and I lost about eighty pounds for all the Guinness we drank.

In bed that night, I thought about the first two days at this job.

The men I worked with were a mixed bag, Tom even-keeled and levelheaded, Angus mentally unstable and just able to function. But I could see why Ian hired him. He would fight himself, the slope, the conditions, the winch, the cables, and the "fuckin' sheep" on the road to complete the job. Overall Angus was dependable, if emotionally erratic. The work itself was beyond anything I'd known, and I'd known hard, dangerous work.

During our morning hauls the next day, Tom's radio went dead. I figured it was completely soaked. Because I was. After lunch we would move the operation.

At lunch, I asked if we had backup radios. The answer was, "Maybe. We can get a backup set from Ian this weekend."

"Are we expected to work without radios?" I asked, looking directly at Angus then Tom.

Standing in the rain with his hood over his head, trying to keep the rain out of his soup, Angus said, "We're expected to get the timber off the slope. That is what we will do. Radios or no radios."

I could see my breath trailing out into the cold, clammy, miserable air. I simply said, "Wow."

We made it to the top in good time, mostly because we wanted to get warmed up again. Once there, Tom instructed me to climb up, undo the main cable, and slip it off without getting my fingers pinched.

I climbed up the tree and shuddered as the rain that had collected on tree branches dislodged and ran down my collar and back.

Tom yelled up. "Next time take a heavy rock and throw it at the tree to knock a lot of that water off the branches."

"Why didn't you tell me that before?"

Lighting another cigarette, he said, "I didn't think about it."

Both physically and emotionally fatigued, I blurted out, "Is there anything easy about this job?"

"Nope. Nothing. Not even payday," he said.

Perplexed at the comment and mad at myself for the weak outburst, I continued. Thankfully, I didn't lose a finger or hurt myself, and I safely made it back to the ground. Chilled again to the bone.

"Does the rain ever stop?" I asked.

Passing me by without missing a step, Tom replied, "Not much."

We did a couple more jobs to move the winch, complete with the struggle and toil, close calls, and constant cold wet I was learning made up most minutes of the workday, and made our way to the car. We switched into our street clothes quickly, drove to the ferry, and got back to Fort William without a word.

I was chilled, tired, and fighting myself in my head, wanting to bail on this entirely unnecessary "lumberjack experiment."

As we pulled up to the hostel, I thanked Angus for the ride.

"Seven-thirty tomorrow," he said, and I nodded, then closed the door.

I took a lot of time to get up the steps at the hostel. When I made it to my room, I headed for the shower. I was worked. Tired mentally and physically.

Showered, still chilled, and hungry, I made my way to the sports store for some shin guards. My mood continued to match the weather. I was depressed, sore, and mad that I'd made the decision to come here and do this work.

I began the job thinking it would be fun and relatively hard. Instead I found it to be hellish on almost every count and brutal for the labor involved, with difficult working conditions (hell, you had to be part squirrel), unsafe work practices, a manic coworker, piss down rain, and perfect hypothermia weather. It all sucked.

As I jumped between mud puddles, my inner dialogue ranged.

"The first week is almost over," I told myself. "It will get easier. And you aren't afraid of working hard and doing dangerous work." Followed by, "What the hell are you thinking? You could easily leave and never see these people again. It's a commitment that you didn't understand."

Back and forth I went as I made my way to the sports store.

They were out of shin guards but I was able to buy an old military sweater made in Scotland and another pair of wool socks. At the register, the man said, "You are going to need these. It's going to get real cold for the next month."

I looked at him blankly. What had it been already? I asked, "Will the rain ever stop?"

"Fuck's sake, no," he replied. "We are in the Highlands, man."

I said nothing while I took off my raincoat and slipped on the sweater. It was not a smooth transition. My soreness must have been obvious.

"You ain't from around here, are you?" he asked.

"Nope," I said.

"What are you doing in these parts?"

"Working in forestry as a lumberjack." I stood there waiting for his response. I still had my sense of humor, which I took as a good sign I wasn't totally defeated.

Dumbfounded, he blurted, "Lumberjack? What the fuck you talking about?"

I ended his misery. "I'm a chokerman."

Still amazed, he asked, "Why the fuck would an American—" He stopped. "You are an American?"

I nodded and he continued. "Why the fuck would an American want to work in forestry as a chokerman?"

Feeling a bit warmer from the sweater inside my raincoat, I replied, "That's what I have been asking myself the last few days. And without some shin guards my shins aren't going to choke anything past next week."

The honesty of my delivery must have landed with the man behind the counter. He softened his expression and leaned forward.

"Come back tomorrow. I'll have a pair for you if I have to give you a pair myself. Fuckin' awful job in forestry. Fuck's sake, man."

His comments jolted me.

I stood stronger, feeling a sense of validation that someone understood how hard the job was. It activated my sense of pride. I was doing an incredibly hard job. And I was a hard worker who had given his word.

My father, as a railroad man, had taught me your word is like the iron tracks that ran through Hornell. The rails never waver; they're always there.

Like our word.

And I knew it was settled. As much as I hated this job, as much as it felt near ridiculous to keep at it, I would stick to my word. I would stay till the end of the season. The argument in my head about leaving was done.

I thanked the man and asked for his name. "Ulten," he said.

"Thank you, Ulten. I'll see you tomorrow."

I made it back to the hostel to cook my pasta and make my lunch for the next day. As I boiled the water and cut up the vegetables, I thought to myself, "You are in this until spring. And the quicker you get right with it, the easier it will be."

My mood didn't change much. I was still slightly chilled, sore, and not looking forward to tomorrow's work. But I did brighten up a bit when I realized I only had one day left in the workweek before two days off.

I read a bit before bed and double-checked my clothes would be dry by morning. I felt glad I'd bought that sweater. I also knew shin guards were on the way. By the time I climbed into bed, with the decision made I would keep working until the end of winter, I fell asleep in a better mood.

The next morning, Tom wasn't in the car. Angus told me he was taking his son to the doctor, but also that from this point, we'd see less of him. "He'll work with us here and there," he said. "But Tom hopes to get a sky winch of his own and do work closer to home. It will be just you and me mostly. We have a lot of work in this area." He nodded at the passing landscape as I registered this unpleasant news. "It's a pretty area when the clouds are gone," he continued, waving his arms around. "Can't see fuck all most of the time, though."

"Yep. It's pretty gray and cloudy," I said.

Angus chuckled. "Gray and cloudy. It's fuckin' depressing."

"Maybe so. But I saw the valley below the lochs. What little I saw the first day was beautiful."

"Yeh… it's beautiful alright. When you can see it. But this weather. It's a fuckin' bitch, man."

After another day much like the others, but without the solid presence of Tom, we knocked off early and got some pints as we waited for the ferry. We drank mostly in silence while we watched the soccer match.

Angus seemed in good spirits. I was just happy the work was over.

Later that night I went to the sports store and sure enough Ulten, the guy behind the counter, had a pair waiting for me. We talked a bit more about my desire to be a "lumberjack," to his great amusement.

I asked him where I should go for a pint, dinner, and some nightlife, and he pointed me in a direction that I had yet to explore. It would become my "regular" stomping ground going forward. That and Paulo and Elsbeth's house.

The weekend went as planned. I spent most of my Saturday working and hanging out with Paulo and his family. The girls loved having me at the house.

Paulo and I talked about my first week and he laughed and laughed. "What did you think you were getting into?" he asked. "Most people that work in forestry either don't like people or people don't like working with them. And it's hard, heavy labor."

The following weeks passed as I'd expected.

Most days, it was just Angus and me. The cold weather soon arrived in force, with everyone talking about the "record lows for the Highlands" we were experiencing. In the increased cold, the felled trees became more slippery and dangerous from the saturated air masses that lifted up from the lochs below.

I tried to zoom in on the bright spots—my time with Paulo's family, and the beauty. The winter sun reflected off the sides of the "mountains" (I would call them large hills) and the ominous, dark blue lochs below were always striking.

My body continued to be sore. Each day or couple of days I had a persistent ache. My ankles were taking a beating and my wrists were nearly raw on the inside. I slept great every night, though.

Angus's mood at work continued to be mostly that of a

maniac. During the drives to and from work he would engage in pleasant conversation or tell me about his marriage problems. Once at the work site he would yell and scream at me, the winch, the trees, the equipment, the hauls, the fact he forgot his cigarettes, and anything else.

Several times we almost came to fists. After one of these incidents, Angus did his best to apologize. "Look, I'm sorry. I get out of line and fucking don't know why. I'll buy you a pint at the ferry."

I laughed at this because he had not bought one pint since I'd met him.

"You can't treat people that way, man. It's not right. No matter what," I said.

Smiling, he said, "Why do you think my teeth are like this?"

I laughed. "OK. You're buying the pints today."

In time Angus and I got into a rhythm. Days remained dangerous. The yelling continued. But I managed.

In the last month, I was able to occasionally work with other crews and met some good men who immediately took me in. "You're alright with us," they would say, "if you can work with Angus these many days without killing him or being killed. Why the fuck do you want to do this work? What did Fergus call it? You want to be a lumber-fucking-jack." A roar of laughter would follow and jokes would be slung my way. However, each of those hardened men said the same thing to me both privately and within the group. "You're a good fucking man for staying. Fergus appreciates it."

Those moments made me proud, helping strengthen my resolve and my confidence that I could work any job, anywhere.

I met with Fergus before I left, this time driving down.

We sat and had a cup of tea in his shop. He was happy with

the work I'd done with Angus, and I thanked him for giving me the opportunity to "be a lumberjack." We both laughed at that.

Looking down at his cup of tea, Fergus asked me, "What will you do now?"

"Take a bus down to Edinburgh. Stay a few days and fly back to the States," I replied.

He said thank you and then handed me my final wages. "Get on your way, before I find a bottle of scotch that needs drinking."

And with that my Highlands lumberjack adventure was over. But it would never leave me.

The funny thing was, when I came to the Highlands, I thought I was a hard worker. I thought I knew the value of integrity. In a lot of ways, I was, and I did. But this was on a whole different level. Now I knew I could work at this level, too, and I knew I would do whatever it took to stand by my word.

During my months in the Highlands, it was as if new layers of growth were taking place inside me. The iron of my integrity and grit had never been tested like they were there on an almost daily basis. I learned that neither weather, maniacs, physical safety, my body giving out, nor simply being dog tired could get me to turn away from the work ethic passed down through four generations of railroaders.

As I left the Highlands, I felt a stronger connection to my own roots and those tracks that I'd never worked on but carried with me. I knew my deepest integrity would be the iron to keep my word. And that was a lesson, and a legacy, I wouldn't take for granted.

CHAPTER 4

Asia: Intention

WE SPEND THE next two days hiking and exploring our surroundings. At times, Ian is overtaken by the hugeness of the landscape—even coming from the front range of Colorado, he often finds the grandeur of Alaska overwhelming. At times he's extremely uncomfortable, and at others, he's giddy with excitement.

It's much the same in our coaching conversations.

As we explore the land, we explore Ian's "map" of his life. Which takes us sometimes far, far into the unknown wild and, ultimately for Ian, into his truth.

After working our legs pretty hard through the morning, we had stopped to "glass" (look for animals) using our binoculars and my spotting scope. We saw Dall sheep high on the mountain peaks, moose down in the valleys, and the occasional bear on the mountain slopes looking for berries that had yet to arrive or ripen. And now we were in pure rest.

"Man, you really have to be intentional to get this far out here," Ian says as he lays back. In what has now become an unconscious movement, he checks his hip to make sure his bear spray is with him. Finding it safe, he shuts his eyes and folds his forearm under his head. He laughs. "And to stay out here."

"True," I say. "Most great journeys, inner or outer, start with intention. It took intention for us to get here. And you've also held intentions for what you wanted from the trip. What you want for your life."

I let my last statement sit for a minute. Then I say, "Earlier I asked you to start taking inventory of your current life." I ease back into my chair and look in Ian's direction. "Care to share some of your insights?"

Ian sits up straighter. He looks up into the wide sky and then turns his windburned face towards me. "Yes, I do."

His emphatic answer seems to surprise him.

I sit quietly, knowing that such responses are usually a sign a client is ready to express something deep or intuitive. I know from experience not to move or offer any comment. To use a coaching term, "I am holding the space for the client." It's in this "space" that a lot of progress, transformation, and realizations can take place.

"Alright," he begins. "Here it is, seriously. It's been a hard go at times and simple at other times. I'll start with the simple stuff first. I love my wife, kids, and family. I'm a husband and father first, that I know to be true. It's also true that I like to be successful. And I'm a hard worker."

Ian continues, "But during our first break about two hours into our hike yesterday, I realized something. I had on a second pair of socks that were causing me huge discomfort. And when I was finally taking them off, after trying to push on because I didn't want to slow us down, I realized I give a lot of my attention to the wrong things. The side issues. In this case wanting to get to the summit quickly. It was stupid to keep going just to save a few minutes. And the truth is at the start of my career I learned to live with the discomforts in order to be successful. I just kept charging forward instead of stopping and examining what was working and what wasn't. Always charging forward." He looks down into the valley to the west.

I only nod. I don't want to offer any words to him as he is talking through his experience.

He continues and I sense he needs to get this out. "Mike, twenty minutes into our hike I knew that having two socks on wasn't going to work. But, stubborn me, I would not stop to fix the issue. I was so fixated on not stopping that I would have continued to hike that way until I had sores on my heels. I only stopped when you stopped. And when I was finally taking off those bloody socks, it hit me that I was an idiot. That when I feel that discomfort, whether physical or anything, I need to simply stop and really ask myself the question you said to me once during coaching. "What is this situation or experience trying to teach me?"

I lean forward, surprised Ian had remembered that question. But then I thought, *I shouldn't be*. Sometimes words come back to someone right when they're ready.

Ian pauses and lightly laughs at the seriousness of his realization. "The uncomfortable truth is I have been living with the discomfort of wearing an extra pair of socks for a long time and it hasn't served me. So it's time to stop and evaluate. Not plow through life. It's time to get rid of the unnecessary pair of socks."

I remain silent and still.

Then Ian breaks the easy silence in his dry English humor. "How's that for a metaphor. Going through life with a worthless extra pair of socks and a foot full of blisters?"

"If it works for you, it works for me, Ian." Looking out in front of us I let the silence build again.

"It was a powerful moment taking those socks off yesterday. But I couldn't really articulate it fully and identify what is unnecessary till now."

"And what is unnecessary?" I ask.

Without hesitation, Ian states, "Staying late and working weekends."

I wait a moment. Then ask, "What else?"

Ian looks away from me and starts to pick at the ground.

I can tell he's starting to get uncomfortable. I wait patiently for him to continue.

He stays quiet but I see his shoulders do an upward kind of shake like when someone begins to sob. As he shakes his head from left to right, he takes a deep breath and says, "I've been choosing work over family and I've missed so much." Gaining his composure he stands up, settles himself, and looks right at me. "I intend it to stop. And it will."

And I believe him.

The timbre of his voice tells me the conversation is over, so I stand up and simply say, "Thank you for sharing."

In typical Ian fashion he forges onward. But this time, I know it's at the right time. "What's the name of these flowers, Mike?"

Putting on my backpack, I say, "Forget me not. It's the state flower."

Ian pulls one out of the ground, takes a moment to reflect, and gently puts it into his journal.

I say nothing but gesture toward the downward slope. Our work at this time and place is done. Ian's found a deep vein of intention, and I know it's the seed of something real.

As we head back down the mountain and I take in the stillness of the rugged beauty, I think back to a similar place of beauty, one where I've seen how much can grow out of intention: the

Altai Mountains region of Western Mongolia, where the Kazakh golden eagle hunters make their home. Where rugged intention is a truth of life.

Ever since I saw that *Wanderlust* cover in the Edinburgh train station, I was driven to learn more about the life I saw captured there. And I soon had the opportunity to do so.

A couple years after my time as a lumberjack, I took a job in Iraq with the military contractor KBR, starting as a crane operator in Babylon and soon moving up to become an operations coordinator. This new position moved me around to small FOBs (forward operating bases) like Karbala and Najef. In all parts of the country, I had great experiences with the Iraqi men, US Department of State, multinational forces, and "spooks" (government people who don't want you to know all of what they're up to—in other words, CIA or something similar).

By then I'd learned that the magazine cover depicted a Kazahk golden eagle hunter, and I began researching the area of Mongolia where they lived. As I did so, I kept seeing the same hunters photographed with the same photographer's name listed over and over in photo credits. I saw he'd even taken the pictures I'd seen in *Wanderlust*.

I made it my mission to find and speak with this man and hire the same guide that he did, so that I, too, could experience this culture. Our time off at KBR came in long stretches—three or four weeks at a time after working three to four months straight—and I wanted to spend my time off in Mongolia, hunting with the Kazahk golden eagle hunters. I just needed to track down this photographer first.

I started asking around.

As operations coordinator, it was my job to know everything going on at the base, and document all things related to "United

States assets." In doing so, I also had to track the fuel supply. One group of spooks were on base a lot for fuel and food, and I struck up a friendship with one of them, who noticed that I also smoked cigars. Soon, we had a habit of drinking "near beer" (nonalcoholic beer) and smoking cigars after dinner on the deck of my office.

One night, halfway through a fine cigar and into my second can of "near beer," I told him about my desire to reach this man and why. I didn't ask him to help me; that would have been rude. A man does not ask anything of another man while smoking a fine cigar. Yet my plight hung in the air with the smoke, and after a couple more puffs and sips, my spook friend simply asked, "What's the name of the book you've been reading about them and who is the author?"

I answered plainly and without emotion. I didn't want to seem too hopeful or uncool. My friend dragged on his cigar and tilted his head as if making a mental note.

The next day after lunch, he came in as he had in the past to get permission for fuel. I obliged and radioed the fuel depot. Afterward, he handed me a piece of paper with the book author's name, address, and phone number, without saying anything. I took it and said, "See you around. Thanks for the company last night."

He spun around and said, "I'll see you when I see you." And with that I had the information that would lead me to the guide.

I was finally able to contact him and book a trip for two. My strong, adventurous, and able Alaskan wrangler friend "Hillbilly Jilly" would join me in this adventure. I flew out of Iraq to Dubai, went through Moscow, and finally landed in Ulaanbaatar (called UB), the capital of Mongolia, where I met up with Jill.

Prior to my trip, I'd read every book I could find about the Kazakh golden eagle hunters (called Sayat in the Kazakh language), Genghis Khan, and the history of Mongolia. It was incredible to think how this nomadic culture started by Genghis Khan created the largest continuous land empire in world history, with a whopping nine million square miles.

In time Jill and I met with our guide, Khanat. He first showed us around Ulaanbaatar, making sure we took in the awe-inducing statue of Genghis Khan and the Buddhist temples. Then the next day we boarded a plane to the extreme western province of Bayan-Olgii, where approximately 80 percent of the world's eagle hunters live and practice their ancient art known as berkutchi.

As we flew the five hundred plus miles to the west, I looked out the window, amazed that I never saw a single paved road on the huge expanse of grasslands. We soon landed on a very small airstrip. A worker on the other side of a six-foot fence lifted our luggage over the fence and unceremoniously let it go without a care, allowing us to grab it if we were ready. It was a new form of luggage chaos I had yet to experience. (One that played hell with people with fragile gear in their bags.)

Hillbilly Jilly, Khanat, and I found our driver/camp boss, named Temji, and our cook, named Boda. We all loaded our gear into an old Toyota Land Cruiser and rumbled up and out of Olgii's valley to what I would call a high plains area, much like South Park, Colorado, on a smaller scale. Mountains encircled us to the north and west while a slight slope led back to Olgii. In the distance there was a small group of brick structures surrounded by the traditional round houses called "gers" in Western Mongolia (and "yurts" farther east).

Temji dodged goats, yaks, Bactrian camels (two-humped), golden eagles tied to wooden perches, and kids as we made our way deeper into what seemed to be a temporary village. In time we stopped and found ourselves being ushered into a dimly lit square house where we were introduced to a family of six lined up in a mass of friendliness. Between us and them was a large circular table filled with meat, cheese, candy, teacups, and other things that I had yet to understand.

We were led to the cushions on the table and offered milk tea with great pride. Of course we took it with great glee. The kids looked at Hillbilly Jilly's blonde hair in amazement. Without missing a beat she gestured to her pigtails and asked the two little girls, "Want to touch them?" In return the girls fought through the adults and their brothers to reach her. (That's why I'd brought her along. She's a beacon for everyone.)

The centerpiece of the meat platter was a burnt goat head of which the mother was especially proud. She had a nice smile with a gold tooth that gleamed as she watched us eat. We each ate a piece of meat from the platter, and once I ate everything off the bone in my hands, the child to my left motioned for me to break the bone in two. I did. The child then motioned for me to suck out the bone marrow. Everyone watched this play to see if I would do it. I simply handed the child one half of the bone, which gave him great delight. He promptly sucked out the "best part" of the meal, as Khanat called it later. His bigger sister looked disappointed, so I handed her the other half.

We continued to eat and wipe our hands on our pants.

Through Khanat, we had polite dinner conversation with the family. We learned that this was their "winter home" and that they traveled with the others to different grazing areas in the spring and summer. The father was proud to speak about his truck and how he could transport two families in one load. The boys were excited to tell us about the fox they trapped for the Eagle Festival.

After dinner we sat around drinking milk tea, eating sweets, and asking and answering questions about the different experiences and landscapes of our lives. Khanat translated the volley of questions and answers. In time I brought out the various postcards of all things Alaska, and the table lit up with excitement and wonder at the pictures, especially those of bears, wolverines, and the ocean.

To cap off the night, I pulled out my Polaroid camera to take a picture of the family. Once my intentions were made clear, the family scurried around the small house to prepare for the picture, making sure they looked their best. When satisfied, they excitedly grouped together, standing straight and tall, hands down to their sides. A gleam of pride and happiness filled the house as they waited for the picture to develop. As the picture took shape, a sense of wonder filled the house. Each family member wanted to hold it once it was complete. As we watched, Khanat turned to Jill. "This is a good gift. They are very happy."

In time we managed to say our goodbyes, pile into the Toyota, and make our short way to our ger for the evening. Inside, Bota had lit the lamp and started a fire in the small square fire box, to heat a pan of water to "wash up" before bed. Our sleeping bags had been rolled out on some furs.

It was all very cozy and welcoming for our tired traveling selves. We slept great.

We were awakened early by Bota starting the fire and making tea. After a breakfast of gruel with a bit of goat's milk, Jill, Khanat, Temji, Boda, and I left for the Eagle Festival. We drove across the flat landscape, joined by people riding their horses, camels, and motorcycles, coming from all directions and heading toward an area nestled up against a few sharp hills in the distance.

As we rolled on toward the focal point, we passed several eagle hunters. I watched riveted as they rode their horses with pride, their eagles stoically perched on their arms. They all wore either a long, neatly embroidered "chapan" overcoat or a long fur coat with a large, oversized collar that hid their faces. On top of their heads fluttered a fox fur hat with large flaps on the right side and a feathered dome in the middle. Thick leather gloves protected their arms, one of which rested on a wooden stick carved into the shape of a "Y." The end of the stick fit snug on the saddle and allowed the hunter and bird to ride relaxed on the small, robust horse, called a "bercut," trained to hunt with a golden eagle.

The eagle wore a small adorned leather hood over its head and eyes, and felt and leather cuffs around both legs, connected by a leather cord held by the hunter to keep the eagle safe. Every once in a while the hunter would lift the eagle into the air, where it would hover aloft like a child's kite.

A low-pressure system created a slight dust cloud near the ground and when the rising sun hit the hunters and their horses, it looked almost as if they were riding on a golden cloud. Almost as if they were riding out of the past. Several times we stopped to admire the almost apocalyptic scene, which some say has been happening for over a thousand years (albeit without the motorcycles).

Everyone was headed for the flatbed trailer, which was used as a stage and center point for the festival. When we reached it, we parked and Khanat gave us a briefing of what was supposed to happen that morning. We were to wander about, "accept any offering of friendship," ride any horse, eat any offered thing, and come back when we saw him standing up on the stage talking.

Khanat finished with a warning. "Be careful about taking those pictures with your camera. People will become excited and then they'll keep following you. They will want pictures. And more pictures," he said. "Pictures of the whole family are very important to the Khazakhs. It is a good gift. But do it silently."

"Got it," I replied.

Our group split up, and I walked up the steep hill, where

several people were sitting near the top, to get a good view of the landscape. Below us was a bustle of activity, with streamers of kicked-up dust flowing out in all directions. The scene reminded me of a jellyfish and its tentacles—it was amazing how alive it all looked.

After taking it in from the top, I made my way down to join in, stopping along the way to say hello to everyone I met. While walking, I noticed a half dozen photographers with cameras strapped across their bodies doing their best to get pictures with the golden eagle hunters. Several times I saw them interrupting what appeared to be old friends deep in conversation. It bordered on rudeness.

As I continued, I happened upon a family that, based on their tears, laughter, and body language, seemed to be reuniting after a long period of time apart. I watched from afar until they had finished their joyful greetings, and then approached with respect and a smile. Through hand signals, more smiles, and gestures to both my cameras (I had a normal one—which at the time meant film—and the Polaroid), I was able to convey what I was offering and wrangle their enthusiasm. They gathered together, and I snapped a Polaroid. I pulled it out, did the customary flipping or airing out of the picture, handed it to the oldest man in the group, and pointed to my watch. "Three minutes," I said. "Wait for three minutes." As the picture formed, the family's excitement grew. When it was ready, they passed it around for all to see. I made a gesture as if it was a gift, and then I asked them to take another picture with my other camera. Which they were happy to do.

As I made my way around the festival, I repeated this experience with several golden eagle hunters and some older women selling their ger embroidery. In time, just as Khanat predicted,

I had a small following. I also gathered an interesting collection of photos.

As I look back on those pictures today, I believe they are so rich with emotion and texture because I first took the time to genuinely interact with the people I wanted to photograph, and more importantly, to give them a gift before asking something of them.

One old woman I photographed even became an ally in my quest to buy a fox fur hat worn by the golden eagle hunters, called a "malakhai." Apparently the hunters have small heads, or I have a big one. To find one that fit me, it took the woman going from eagle hunter to eagle hunter asking—but really telling—them, "Let me see your hat." They complied without a thought, and she would hand it to me to try on. At first we laughed together. In time it became a bit exhausting. But we did prevail, eventually finding two hats that fit. With Khanat's help, I paid her a "fair price" in US dollars. She was the broker of the deal, after all. (And I still have the hats.) I also found an ankle-length fur coat I was excited to take home.

There were various other activities happening in different places around the festival, like archery, horseback tug-of-war—using a dead, gutted goat with a sandbag stuck inside the carcass—and a long-distance horse race. Another fun activity was where a man tried to "steal a kiss on horseback" from a woman cracking her whip at him, to the delight of the crowd.

Then in time, the eagle hunter competition began. The eagle hunters lined up two by two for what seemed like a parade in front of everyone. The air filled with the sound of people clapping, eagles chirping, and expensive camera shutters capturing the procession. Then the eagle hunters each hiked or rode their sturdy horse to the top of the sharp hill above us. They would gently put the eagle on a rock facing the valley, whisper a command to "stay" to the eagle, and ride or hike back down to the crowd, where a circle was outlined on the ground. Once they stepped inside the circle, they would call the bird.

The hunters were judged on how many times they called the birds and how long it took the eagles to fly from their perch to the hunters. A well-trained eagle will respond to the first call and fly directly to the hunter. A not-so-well-trained eagle will not respond immediately and when it does, will circle and circle before eventually returning to the hunter. The winner of the competition got to send his eagle to a fox tethered to a stake in the center of the circle, for the kill.

As the festival and day unfolded, I continued to take Polaroids and give them away. Jill decided to enter the horseback tug-of-war competition—and much to the delight of the crowd she won! By the end of the day, I think she and I were the most popular people there.

After the festival ended, our group returned to the car and went to get more supplies. Then our full party rode to meet two golden eagle hunters on the outskirts of town, one older and the other younger. The younger hunter's name translated as "Dream Boy," and he spoke a bit of English. Khanat had arranged for us to ride with them back to their family ger, a three-day ride away into the "valley of the white rock."

Jill and I looked over our horses and tack before mounting up. The saddle was made of four components: bent rebar fashioned into the shape of the saddle, four sanded boards attached to the rebar that ultimately touched the horse, a set of leather straps with rebar-fashioned stirrups, and a square cushion to sit on. The cushion was literally a couch pillow.

I asked Khanat how I was supposed to adjust the stirrups, since the leather was in a very old knot. Plainly and void of any emotion, Khanat answered, "You're not."

"This will be interesting," I said. And it was.

While the saddles were less than ideal, the horses themselves were beautiful.

Mongolian horses are considered the native breed of Mongolia, one that's believed to be unchanged since the time of Genghis Khan. They have a stocky build, and are known for their stamina, large heads, self-sufficiency, and incredible easygoing manner. These horses were the engine of Genghis Khan's empire-building machine.

Prior to mounting our horses, I lit a fine cigar and moved upwind of the horses to make sure my cigar smoke didn't spook them. In my years of riding horses, I've learned it's better to introduce the smell upwind where horses can see where the smell and smoke are coming from. Since using this method, I haven't been bucked off once.

I settled onto my horse peaceably, and we set out into the vast brown-and-gray landscape. Far in the distance, the mountains held a light touch of snow on their peaks. Sweeping inclines connected the mountains to a flat valley below made of gravel and stubby grass. It was wide open, breezy, and silent. It was magnificent.

With the ankle-length fur coat and fox fur hat I'd bought at the festival, I was very warm and felt I looked the part (that is, if Kazakhs smoked cigars). My horse and I got along fine. My long legs and shorts stirrups did not. Although they did at least offer a temporary resting spot for my feet once my legs were near-totally numb from dangling off the side of the horse.

We rode in a pack. Mostly quiet, each of us drinking in the landscape and the whisper of the wind. The older hunter would sometimes join the music of the wind with a gentle song directed at the eagle. The song, with the sway of the horse's gait and the gentle rhythm of the hunter's hand on the eagle, brought us into an atmosphere of respect and love.

I would experience this congruence of man, eagle, nature, and more than five centuries of tradition over and over during my time with the hunters. Sometimes a song and sometimes a chant would allow this feeling to emerge, one that seemed to bear witness to the remarkable bond between the eagle, known to the Kazakhs as the "King of the Sky," and their human master.

These moments of harmony were the beginning of my truly understanding the depth of intentional interaction between eagle hunters (and their families) and their eagles. As our time together continued, I was lucky to understand it more and more.

The Kazakh people hold the golden eagle in the highest regard. And it is an incredible bird, with a wingspan of up to eight feet and a maximum diving speed well over 150 miles an hour.

Although the eagle's life expectancy is up to forty years, an eagle hunter will only keep one for eight to ten of those before releasing it back into the wild. The night before the release, the eagle hunter has a large party where his family and neighbors come to hear stories of the pair's time hunting together. In the morning, the hunter will take a dead goat and ride with the eagle for the last time, far from their home high into the mountains. There, the hunter will drop off the eagle with the goat left as food, wait until dark, say their goodbyes, and pray. Then leave in the cover of darkness.

It ends with ritual. As it begins.

Hunters most often learn the various practices of eagle hunting from their father, who learned from their father, going back centuries. Each ritualized action is an act of respect to the generations of eagle hunters before them. It's their connection to the past.

To be worthy of this ancient bond to ancestors and eagle, a hunter must first capture an eagle, a process that can take months.

As I was told, one way to capture an eagle is by using bait—a captive raven—and a handwoven net held upright by seven sticks. Eagles dislike ravens and will swoop down to scare them and capture the bait. When this happens, the net falls on the eagle.

Another way to capture an eagle is to search the high Altai Mountain crags and peaks for nests. Once a nest is located, a hunter can climb up and capture a young eagle directly. When talking about this method, eagle hunters always cross their index fingers to reference the eagle back feathers. This represents the age in which the eagle is ready to be taken.

Or, a hunter can find where an eagle nests and place a lot of meat as bait where the eagle will find it. In time, the eagle will arrive and gorge itself on the meat, so much that it won't be able to fly away. The hunter, hiding within eyesight of the bait, can then throw a net over the eagle and claim it as their own.

The process is a crucible that deepens the connections to past and present generations of eagle hunters, establishes the intentions of the new hunter, and honors the enormity of the task, all before the bond with the eagle has even begun.

The time and energy it takes to capture an eagle weeds out the faint at heart. Thus, there are just over four hundred Kazakh eagle hunters in Mongolia. While this group has historically been all men, today ten of this number are women.

Training the eagle requires the same intentional efforts. First, the eagle is brought home, welcomed in like a treasured new family member. It's given the most sacred area of the ger, where it perches on a wooden block or pole called a "tugir." As part of domesticating the bird, the hunter binds its feet with handcrafted leather-and-felt cuffs that are connected by an ornately braided leather strap. Attached to the strap is a four-foot braided cord for the hunter to hold on to. The cords, straps, and cuffs are beautifully detailed and strong, works of art and a link to hunters throughout history.

Honoring the link to past generations runs through an eagle hunter's every practice. It is an intentional form of believing in themselves, their ancestors, the bond between hunter and eagle, and the way of life it requires. It's their identity.

Training, a process that takes three to four years, begins with the eagle learning to be fed by only his master. He is fed one lean cup of meat each day, which the hunter prays over as he prepares. As it eats, the hunter speaks to the eagle about its strength and how they will become great hunters together. Eventually, the hunter releases the eagle to capture on command a fox or rabbit pelt being dragged a short distance on the ground. As the training continues, so does the trust between hunter and eagle, and so does the distance.

Throughout our three-day ride, we got to witness the eagles respond to the commands of the hunters, and it was a sight to see. As one called to their eagle, it would spring into action high into the air, chirping all the while as it returned to his master's glove. Once back in place, the hunter would feed the eagle a piece of meat as it was being praised. I greatly looked forward to embarking on an actual hunt with them after we reached our destination.

When we arrived at the hunters' village, everyone came out to greet us and we were immediately given a bowl of milk tea. The children played with Jill and helped remove saddles as they giggled and dared each other to touch one of her blonde pigtails. She hammed it up with them, to the delight of onlookers.

Later in the day the evening chores began. The hunter's wife tied up the goats to be milked, before one was presented to the elder eagle hunter to be killed in our honor for the evening meal. Everyone prayed before the life was taken with a respectful cut to its neck. A plastic tub was used to collect the blood and the "guts" were collected into another plastic container.

A small child helped his mother by starting a fire nearby. The head of the goat would be roasted over the fire with the meat.

Once everything was complete, we all entered the ger to be seated around the short table. The platter of meat, intestines, and goat head in the centerpiece were placed on the table with great reverence and excitement. After the prayer, the hunter handed me a knife and instructed me to cut a square of skin off the charred skull and eat it. According to Khanat, this was an honor.

With everyone's eyes on me, I gulped down the burnt skin.

Jill and I were handed the "good parts" to eat, and the kids fought over the broken bones for the tasty treat of bone marrow. Which they sucked out with great delight.

After the dinner we washed our hands, returned to our seats, and were presented with a cup of airag, fermented mare's milk. It had a slightly sour taste but it was agreeable enough to drink one cup. (Two cups was pushing it.) So, I drank slow.

The hunter played his dombra, a traditional Kazakh stringed instrument, and throat sang for us. I was told the songs were a mixture of his own eagle hunting stories and songs of years gone by.

After all the dishes were cleared away, the hunter took us outside to watch him feed his eagle. Again, he prayed over the meat, unhooded the eagle, and sang to him as he fed him. Afterwards he stroked him with great care and told him that tomorrow we would hunt for "whatever our eyes fall upon." With that he brought the eagle inside the ger for the night.

We all returned to the ger, where our bedding had been laid

out by Bota. We were told that everyone would be going to bed soon so "please prepare to sleep." Which we did. Outside as we brushed our teeth, Jill and I made a mental note of where the "bathroom" was in case the airag did not settle. Khanat wished us well. He would be sleeping in another ger.

The following morning, we awoke to the woman of the ger stocking the dried dung fire in the small fire box. Jill and I lazily lay in until the woman motioned to us our milk tea was ready, then we dressed, drank our tea, and ate a simple breakfast.

We walked outside to find clear morning sunshine. We were ready to start our hunt.

As Khanat, Jill, and I saddled up and rode out of camp with the hunters of the ger, another older eagle hunter and several young boys joined us.

I recognized the approaching older eagle hunter from the festival. I had taken his picture with his eagle.

That morning, like at the festival days before, his eagle wore a bright orange feather on his back between his wings, and he himself wore a full white fur coat. His face at rest looked serious and stoic, yet when he smiled, it took up half his face and revealed his true self as a kind man with a jovial outlook on life. He held himself with kindness and reverence, and everyone showed him great respect. Later I learned he was the Mullah of the Valley.

I had instantly taken a liking to him at the festival and was now glad to see him again.

He spoke, his voice muffled and coming more out of his nose than his mouth. (Only when he laughed would he sound clear.)

Khanat translated what the old eagle hunter said. "Yntan said he is happy to see you. He said you are generous and kind."

I stopped in my tracks and looked Yntan in the eye. I gave a slight bow and slowly covered my heart with my right hand. "Thank you," I said.

We rode in silence for most of the morning, up a steep ridge. Jill and I were both struck with how incredibly sturdy and strong the horses were, to be able to climb and maneuver over the rocks. My guide horse back in Alaska would never have been able to make it. Let alone with me on its back.

The young boys dismounted at various stages of the ridge and the horses continued on with us. Once at the top we dismounted, spread out, and waited for the young boys to start walking across the ridge making noise and throwing rocks. They were now called "scare boys," with the job of scaring game out into the valley below.

As they did this, the eagle hunters unhooded their eagles, which put them in a state of high alert. You could tell just by the jerky motions of their heads. Periodically the hunter would stroke and softly speak to the eagle, as it sat upon their forearm.

Once the scare boys made it to the end of the ridge, we would mount up, meet them with their mounts, and ride down into the valley together. Sometimes an eagle hunter would leave their eagle at the top and call it to him once he made it to the valley below.

This is how we hunted.

After midday prayer, we ate a simple lunch of dried meat. Then we began to circle back toward our hosts' ger via the other side of the valley ridge, using the same system of hunting.

Later in the day, the scare boys managed to flush out a red fox. The fox ran out into the valley headed for the other side, and the eagle saw it immediately, chirping in excitement and bobbing his head up and down. Yntan spoke firmly to his eagle and sent it into the air.

We watched with quiet anticipation as the eagle quickly flapped his wings to get up to speed and gain altitude. The fox was hauling ass making a straight line for the nearest rock—it had about one hundred yards to go before the eagle began his dive toward his moving prey—then quickly turned to the right. It must have sensed or heard the eagle above. Yet the eagle effortlessly made the correction and began to prepare his body and talons for the high-speed impact.

The eagle's talons hit the fox from the right side and the fox turned into the eagle, trying to fight back. The bird's outstretched wings, which helped it keep balance, blocked our view of the scene. We saw wings flapping a couple of times, and in time the fox's movements became less violent and numerous.

Yntan was calm during this ancient act of hunter and prey playing out before us. I was honored to witness the results of his hard work and dedication to his chosen way of life.

We made our way down to the eagle and dead fox.

The eagle looked at his master as he chirped and held on to the fox in his talons. As Yntan approached, he gently spoke. I could tell they were words of praise, gratitude, and respect.

After feeding the eagle with meat he had in his pouch, Yntan put the eagle's hood back on.

Khanat explained it was a "good kill" because the eagle was not injured by the fox and the eagle did not tumble, or "make wrestle," with the fox. Also, the fact that the eagle did not tear into the fox pelt with his sharp beak was a sign of his training.

I congratulated Yntan with a nod and smile. He responded in kind.

Before we mounted our horses to ride back to the village, I lit up a fine Plasencia cigar. "In honor of the kill and the hunter's eye and swift action," I said.

Yntan nodded as the blue smoke gently faded into the light breeze.

He, Khanat, and I rode side by side across the wide valley

back to the ger. As we rode, I asked questions about the training of the eagle, and Khanat translated.

"How long have you been an eagle hunter?" I asked Yntan.

Khanat relayed my question.

Before the eagle hunter answered he sat a bit straighter in the saddle, his body language showing me he was proud of his answer. His words came out in his native language and then Khanat spoke. "Since I was a boy. My father taught me, and his father taught him. This goes on beyond memory."

Before asking the next question, I first held a space of respectful silence to match the reverence of his answer.

Then I spoke again. "How often do you train together?"

Yntan stroked the eagle. It felt as if he was speaking for them both. Like they were one and the same. "Every day, I feed and care for her. I fly her every other day. We train mostly in the mornings when the animals are most active. We hunt at least three times a week. So... the eagle flies almost every day. She must stay strong."

"Will you tell me about how you got her?" I asked.

"I spent many days looking for the right nest," he said. "When I found it, I climbed up, but she was not ready to be taken." Yntan brought his two index fingers together but did not cross them, representing an eagle who is still too young.

"What did you do then?"

As Khanat translated my words to Yntan, the hunter chuckled.

Then again his words came back to me through Khanat. "Ha ha. Nothing. I watched, and waited. It took a long time of waiting. But it's been worth it. She is a strong eagle."

Yntan smiled, his nose and cheeks pushing up against his oversized glasses. "I started training her once I could get the hood over her eyes and fit the leather on her legs. After that she calmed down over two days. When she became hungrier than she was mad I could feed her and show her that I was her master. I spent the first two weeks just talking with her about what we would do together. I sang to her too."

"May I ask what you sang to her about?"

Yntan laughed, and chuckled out the words for a good long time. Khanat didn't begin to translate until Yntan was done because he too was laughing.

"I sang to the bird not to hurt me. I said, I will take care of you as if you were my child. I communicated to her like my father did with his eagle and before that… I sang that I believed in her strength and good eyes. I sang songs of past hunts with my other eagles. But not much… I didn't want her to get jealous."

The laughter held in the breeze as we rode into the wind. In time the wind began to get stronger, and I started to take pictures of Yntan and the group. To make more conversation, I turned to Yntan and said, "Windy."

He grunted through his nose and stuck it up as if to say, "This is nothing." At that very moment, a fresh gust of wind blew over us and pushed his eagle into his face. This led to a quick camera click from me, and muffled laughter from underneath the eagle.

Through the smiles and laughter, Yntan spoke to Khanat. "Don't show that to anyone. I am supposed to be a great eagle hunter."

At that, we all laughed.

That evening I asked Yntan about releasing the eagle back into the wild.

Khanat translated without pause, and a stillness came over the room. I immediately thought that I'd asked the wrong question.

Then Yntan spoke. "I will release this eagle like all the others. My heart will be grateful and heavy all at the same time. As I ride to release her, I will sing or tell her stories. I will feed her for the last time and wait for darkness to come while keeping my heart happy for her. I will take off the leather and say my last thoughts and hopes to her as I remove the hood. She will pay no attention to me because she will be eating at the dead goat. Then I will leave. It is always hard but my heart stays bright for each one of them."

His face was both bright and sad as he spoke. The bottom of his oversized glasses served him well, keeping back the tears. He paused, then continued. "I think of them all often. They are like our children."

His wife stood up, tears on her cheeks, and went to get some candy and tea.

When she returned, I thanked her. Then I turned to Yntan, slightly bowed my head, looked him in the eyes, and said thank you.

He smiled and lifted his cup of tea.

I spent two weeks hunting with various golden eagle hunters and more than twenty-one days overall in Mongolia. The time spent with these incredible people was a gift.

Through it, I came to understand that the golden eagle hunters commit to much more than hunting for fur and meat. They hunt to also preserve their legacy and traditions that are bigger than the "big sky above." Their families make a commitment, too, and together their individual actions collectively preserve a way of life.

It's a big vision, and realizing it requires a deep intentionality. Which I saw through everything the Khazakh golden eagle hunters did—from how they saved the best lean meat for the eagle to how they gave it the best space in the ger. Their whole lifestyle is a chosen one of intention—built around the intention to find, train, hunt, and care for the eagle and ultimately release it back into the wild.

As I lived with and observed the eagle hunters, I absorbed the beauty of their living so completely with intention. I knew it was something I would take forward with me into my own life, as I moved to realize my own vision. I also knew I would pass this understanding to others.

Yntan said to me once while we were out hunting, "I made this decision not only for me, but my family, my ancestors, and the next generations. It's the right choice inside me that I live every day and every season."

It was, and is, a noble choice.

When I would look into the shadows of the ger and see the eagle's regal stare, I saw generations of intentionality reflected back at me. And I was honored with the sight.

CHAPTER 5

Antarctica: Emotional Intelligence/Awareness

IAN AND I are at the tail end of a full-day hike, our last of this trip. We've made our way through the short taiga and the squishy tundra to the top of the mountains across from our camp.

It's breathtakingly beautiful. And a little savage.

The wind is whipping past our ears, loud and powerful enough we have to raise our voices to hear each other. It's also powerful enough to sometimes pull the breath right out of us—which can be a little scary, especially if you haven't experienced something like it before.

I can tell Ian is starting to feel slightly panicked. I call this "weather stressed."

It's not uncommon for people to get overwhelmed by roaring wind on a high peak, especially one so far away from camp. When this happens, their instinctive thought is to want to just get back down, quickly. Yet, the quickest way down is usually not the way we came. And it wasn't today either.

"We're going to walk down the ridge over there," I say, pointing.

He nods, and I continue as we walk.

"We're going to 'step down the scree' of rocks. It's kind of like skiing, but not." I show him what I mean, leaning far back into the mountain and letting the sliding action carry me down. When I stop, I turn back to look at him. "Try it."

Ian shakes his head. "I know you love your challenges, Mike, but can't we find a better way?"

"Admittedly, it's not comfortable at first, but trust me, this is the better way. And you'll get good at it after a few minutes." I slide down another stretch to prove my point. "It's all about letting go and just going with it."

He still isn't having it. "Mike, you're gonna kill me."

I laugh. "I'm definitely not gonna kill you. Instead, I'm gonna talk with you through this, and you're going to do great," I say. "It's all about finding the rhythm of the scree slide. We start with a sense of what we're going to do—lean back, slide down—and then, like with life, we stay aware and respond to the feedback we feel."

He still looks dubious, but less so. I can see I'm starting to convince him.

"Just follow my lead. Lean back, keep your feet moving, adjust as needed, and enjoy the experience." With that, I surf down the mountainside scree for another two hundred yards.

When I look back, I'm satisfied to see Ian stepping into his first slide.

I make it through the scree and find a comfortable spot to wait for Ian, my feet kicked out in front of me. Purple forget-me-not flowers are all around, and I admire the view. We're still high above the valley floor.

A short minute later, Ian's caught up, too, one-quarter

grumpy and three-quarters ecstatic. I stay seated and he comes to sit next to me. We are out of the major wind and we can now talk more quietly.

"Holy shit, Mike, that was mental," he says.

"Yep, it can be. But what was more 'mental' for you?" I ask. "The height, the wind, or the weight of your reluctance to just go with the scree?" I catch his eyes, smile, and then look back to the small flowers wiggling in the wind.

"Ah, come on, Mike! Can't I just rest for a minute without the deep questions?" He takes a long drink from his water bottle and cracks a smile.

"Deep questions are a part of the deal, Ian. No escaping them." I pull out two cigars, cut the ends, and hand him one. "But I'm a civilized guy. Think it through with a fine Plasencia cigar made by my friends, the Plasencia family of Esteli, Nicaragua."

We light the short "robosto"-sized cigars and the blue smoke rises and swirls in the air, dancing in the light.

I settle into my sitting position to enjoy the cigar, the view, and the dancing of the blue smoke as I wait for Ian to comment on his "scree surfing" experience.

Time passes and then he says, "That conversation yesterday was pretty intense for me. I needed that. Thank you."

"You are welcome," I respond.

"It took being out here in this huge expanse without the day-to-day distraction to get to that realization that I truly feel inside me. Like in my core. A feeling that something has changed or shifted."

His tone of voice is one that is familiar to me but I ask him about it anyway, to bring certainty, to him and me. "I notice that your tone of voice changed in your last comment. Who are you being when you say something in that tone of voice?"

Ian stares out across the valley, pauses, and then answers.

"I'm being someone who's recognized a change in who I am. In the past, when I've used that tone of voice it's a done deal. It's hard to explain…" He pauses again, wrestling the feeling into words. "I guess I discovered a truth, the truth that I need to be more present and intentional in life, and how I said it showed how things had reshuffled in me because of it. I know it's going to change things. I know I'm changing, for the better."

I continue to quietly send gentle sheets of blue smoke across the mountainside and let Ian continue to work through his experience in his own way on his own time.

We pass the time in silence enjoying the view and the fine cigars. When we are nearly finished with our cigars, Ian stands up, stretches, and takes a drink of water. Refreshed, satisfied, and far more relaxed than when we first arrived in our spot.

"Alright, Mike. I know you aren't gonna let me not answer your question of 'What was mental about coming down the mountain like that?' Well here is my answer so we can get moving again. Judging on how comfortable you look sitting there, you're not leaving until the question is answered," Ian says with a laugh. "Am I right?"

I nod and match his laugh. "That or till I get cold or uncomfortable."

As Ian puts on his pack he declares his answer. "Coming down the side of the mountain was a metaphor of how I will need to live or 'be'"—he looks directly at me both in jest and seriousness—"the change of being more present and aware and intentional in life. I can't control how life unfolds but I can go with it and not fight it. I can choose my steps accordingly."

I begin to sit up. "Nice, Ian. And what else?"

"Fuckin hell, Mike. I hate when you say that. The 'what else is' stop forcing everything or storming into all of life. Be intentional but also lean back, enjoy what's happening at the moment, and make adjustments as needed toward my goals."

Slinging my backpack on my shoulders I say loud enough that Ian can hear me, "Great work, Ian. That's really good stuff right there and—"

Ian cuts me off. "Well I am a rocket scientist."

I laugh with him and start walking but not without finishing my last statement. "Excellent work, Ian. Now start thinking about how you are going to do all that you said up here. But just think on it. We can discuss it later."

Ian raises his hand as if to wave me off. "Yeh yeh yeh… I know, Mike. I know."

I draw several more times to get the most out of the cigar. The blue smoke keeps swirling in the wind.

There's something familiar about it. And then I remember. Another time seeing this same movement of blue smoke, my feet kicked out in front of me. The difference was they were propped up on a desk that day. My attitude was a little different, too.

At the time, I had yet to really learn all of what Ian and I had just covered back there. Staying aware of my environment—in this case my emotional one—and making adjustments as needed. But that lesson came soon enough.

I was sitting in a lonely one-window container in the middle of the Iraqi desert, interviewing to work in Antarctica as a cargo handler. My feet kicked up in front of me. Blue cigar smoke drifting in front of me and catching the light.

As I exhaled, I felt exhilarated, both with a sense of being able to do anything and by the prospect of working on the "ice" of Antarctica. The interviewer and I got along great. My answer to a lot of questions was simply, "Yep, I can do that."

Not only did I get the job but I was offered the position of lead cargo handler.

I arrived at McMurdo Station in Antarctica like everyone else—excited, wearing a big red parka, and needing to pee. The C-17 US military cargo plane was not equipped with bathrooms needed for all 150 passengers. It's a cargo aircraft after all. And it's pretty damn uncomfortable, too. But I—again, like everyone else—quickly forgot that once we stepped out the aircraft door into the bright sun shining at the bottom of the world.

The experience was unlike anything else I've known.

I stood mouth agape, bladder full, and eyes straining to take in the colors—stark white, deep blue, and volcanic black. Also, the lack of color. Because on the ice, there aren't many of them.

There's also not much smell, beyond yourself, with no trees or flowers, and very little of anything manmade. Cold does not smell. It's just cold. Maybe that is also part of why the colors are so intense.

The scene is so striking the ground crew literally had to push us forward, a line of red parkas slowly moving, smiling, sometimes crying, and taking pictures. Those were my first happy moments on the ice. They would linger the next day through the mandatory orientation, safety meetings, and introductions.

Soon, I had a few other impressions, too. It was immediately clear that living arrangements were very close (I had three roommates), there was an abundance of and big interest in alcohol (they had something like a liquor store and also three different bars), and work and life were literally on top of each other here (everyone was called first by the department they worked for and then their name; I was "Cargo Mike").

Living and working together so closely, I knew the importance of making a good impression on everyone. *Basically, don't be a jerk*, I told myself. *Just be cool and easygoing, and everything else will be fine.*

After I arrived, I met up with a great friend of mine from Alaska, who laid the social scene out for me. Gary was intelligent, a loner, a bit of a "strange cat," and very experienced on the ice. He'd worked there for over fifteen seasons.

"OK, here it is," Gary said in a matter-of-fact way. "Get yourself a girlfriend before the Halloween party. If you don't, you'll be lonely the rest of the season. People around here seem to shack up fast. Not much available after Halloween."

Half bewildered, I simply nodded in the affirmative.

Gary continued. "Who you are at work is equally important as who you are off work. Word gets out pretty quick around here. Do your best to keep a happy-go-lucky perception of yourself. If you do, you'll get invited to parties. Nothing is worse than knowing about a party here and not being invited. It gets lonely really quick."

I nodded again. "Thanks, Gary," I said. "Anything else I should know?"

Gary's eyes darted around the large two-tiered cafeteria before he spoke. "Well… this place is strange. We're all locked on the ice for five months, eating the same food, seeing the same people. It gets old. It's a crazy social experiment marathon with work and booze down here. So easy does it, Mike. Easy does it."

I let it all sink in. "Got it," I said, and he darted off.

I'm a likeable guy and a hard worker. It would be simple enough, I thought.

My fall into work and social purgatory happened, though, on my first real day on the job.

That morning, all the newly flown-in cargo handlers met at the cargo bay building. Several of them had years of experience on the ice, and a few of us were brand new. We were all in good spirits.

The shift supervisor, a good-hearted man named Bear, gathered us all up for a day of orientation to equipment, vehicles, and procedures. Several of the ice veterans made passive-aggressive remarks that I registered, like, "Oh, you are the new 'lead.'" With quotation marks fairly clear in their voice. But for the most part, we exchanged easy, nice banter back and forth while moving around in a gaggle of red parkas or heavy cargo jackets.

We started outside getting an overview of the heavy equipment, mainly the big cargo haulers, cargo scales, and work area. Afterward, we returned to the warmer cargo bay to go over the aircraft pallets, cargo nets, and chains. Bear had set up a large aircraft pallet with a large wooden box in the center, topped with a whiteboard and markers. A cargo net, racket straps, and pile of chains were off to the side.

Bear called us around the pallet. "Alright, let's spend some time getting to know or getting reacquainted with the basics of our trade. I'm standing on an aircraft pallet and the D-rings." Using his foot, he pointed them out. "Five on one side, six on the other. Now this is a box of cargo, and there is a cargo net. Great."

A guy named Seth was standing next to the pile of racket straps.

"Seth, could you hand me a racket strap, please?" Bear asked.

Seth handed the strap.

"Great, thank you. This racket strap, also called a load strap or tie-down strap, is your friend. Treat it like one. Remember to feed the other end of the strap through the inside barrel of the ratchet." He turned to me. "Mike, can you please hand me a chain?"

I sprang into action. Dutifully responding without thinking, I quickly bent down and grabbed the six-foot chain with two hands. As I stood up, I noticed the chain only had one clevis hook at one end. And again without thinking, I shared the observation. While I turned to hand Bear the chain, I exclaimed to the whole group, "This chain only has one clevis hook."

The eyes and dropped jaws of those with years of cargo experience said it all. And Bear almost dropped the tie-down. It reminded me of *The Little Rascals*, when Spanky saw or heard something that he just could not believe. The silence was awful.

I stood there holding the chain out to Bear, but he was too shocked to take it. Two experienced cargo handlers turned away. One walked away with his head shaking.

I advanced one step to Bear to break the awkward silence and handed him the chain.

Still stunned, he simply said, "Thank you."

When I stepped back into the group, people slowly moved away as if I had just farted. I began to get really uncomfortable.

Still taken aback, Bear began again slowly, "Yeah… so a chain binder will attach itself to the end of the chain without the hook." He was recovering his senses and did his best to move on. "Now I need three volunteers to secure this piece of cargo to this aircraft pallet, using straps and a cargo net. I'll be right back."

The group quickly moved away from me, either to work on the job Bear had given us or to stand at the side and talk about what just happened. I felt in the middle of developing choreography for a sitcom.

Standing there alone, I thought about what just happened. I felt like I was in a free fall.

I finally landed in reality. I knew this was the result of my cocky inflation during the interview, i.e., my lack of emotional intelligence. I was overwhelmed with emotions—embarrassed over what had happened, frightened by how quickly I felt isolated from the group, and unsure about what do to or what was going to happen next.

I stood there in a very awkward state until I didn't want to stand alone anymore. I wandered over to the group, which by their body language wasn't feeling all that welcoming.

A woman named Kai came to my rescue by making space. Even though it was uncomfortable, I did my best to help the group finish a job that only two people were needed to accomplish. The more experienced cargo handlers were holding their own private lessons on the different aspects of the tools of the trade. I grabbed a strap just to have something to hold on to until Bear came back.

When Bear returned, he inspected the work of the group. We'd done a nice job of securing the load. He gave us a break to "do whatever you need to do" before instructing us to meet back in twenty minutes.

Everyone scrambled away from me. I headed to the bathroom and to get a cup of hot tea.

I spent the remainder of the day doing my best to learn, help, and interact with the group as a productive member. I was met with mostly cold kindness by the experienced cargo handlers, but the others were a bit more welcoming.

Finally, the day ended. I had half expected Bear to pull me aside and speak with me before sending us off, but he didn't. Nor did he do so the next couple of days of "group orientation," which made it even more uncomfortable. He just continued to speak to me in front of others as if I were the "cargo lead." Since, technically, I was.

When it was time to split into our different groups, one of which I would lead, I was given a very diverse group of individual workers. Basically I was given several experienced cargo handlers who had a lot of skill but didn't always work well with others.

We came to be known as the "misfits and renegades." Which in my opinion was very accurate.

I had three individuals with strong ideas on how things were or should be done, one seeming stoner who was not actually a stoner, and one go-to person who often worked harder at aligning the group than she (being new to the ice) should have. A somewhat motley bunch of big personalities that liked to do things their way with two easygoing, hardworking people hungry to be successful. With me as their "lead."

After being broken up into teams, we were forced to get things done.

One such thing was taking care of cargo from the inbound C-17 aircraft from Christchurch, New Zealand, which needed to be unloaded, inventoried, and stored for later unpacking and possible repacking to the South Pole. Then the empty outbound C-17 aircraft needed to be reloaded with cargo headed back. This job required a lot of strategic planning, radio communication, and follow-through, mostly while operating heavy equipment. There were important moving parts, fragile cargo, expensive equipment, tight timelines, and very little room for things to go wrong. We would have to work together. Thankfully, Bear provided a high-level overview of what needed to be done when. No one dared question his directives. I was left to see that it got done in a safe and timely manner.

Although our group had a lot of experience and hard workers, it was difficult to get aligned as a team or simply complete tasks as we agreed during our team meetings. For example, a new cargo handler would often be paired up with an experienced one. During our group meetings it would be decided who would do what tasks and when, yet later when I would make my rounds to check on progress I would find out the experienced cargo handler chose to do the task differently. Our conversation around it would sound something like this.

Me: "I thought we agreed to do this job this way. Why are you doing it differently?"

Cargo handler with more experience: "Because I knew my way was better." Normally this would be coupled with an attitude of "What do you know?"

When we broke for lunch and went to the mess hall, I often ate by myself. I started reading a book to keep me company. At the end of the workday, I often found myself walking back to the housing area alone, too.

Our group didn't really hang out together off hours. Other cargo teams seemed to do the opposite.

Each week I learned more about being a cargo handler, yet each week my team and I became more and more frustrated. Although we were able to complete our daily tasks and missions, it was not fun. Thankfully, we eventually had another group join us, from the New Zealand Air Force troops. Much like most Kiwis, they were laid back and did what was asked of them.

They were led by a middle-aged female lieutenant, Lieutenant Biggins, who did a great job keeping her troops out of my team's turmoil and keeping the general mood laid back. At times I could see her bite her tongue regarding the drama. By the end of the workweek, we were all ready to get away from each other. Thank God we had two days off.

The weeks dragged on to the night of the Halloween party. Like many new-to-the-ice folks, I was left to rummage through the left-behind and recycled costumes from years past. I managed to find a far-too-small off-color leotard and long blond wig. I can't say the look came together that well for me, but still, the Halloween party was even better than it was talked up to be.

There were creative and amazing outfits, and everyone seemed to have a good time.

The party eventually died out and people went to their separate "private parties," none of which I was invited to. I got back to my room late, buzzed, and bummed that I wasn't still out partying.

The weeks turned into months of more of the same—our just-barely performing team, isolation, and basic dread for me.

We had moved our operations out to the Pegasus Airfield because the ice runway had melted, and the US Coast Guard icebreaker created a channel for a supply vessel from California to dock and unload supplies. This meant we had to drive our large and slow cargo-carrying trucks to and from the airfield, a trip that took upward of forty minutes in good conditions. The distance of the drive added additional stress to the operations. Since very sensitive cargo could only be outside in the elements for short periods of time, we had to coordinate with the flight tour, planes, and other departments. Our team had to function at a high level of performance, and as a result, my stress level would often raise to a high level, too, and stay there. It was uncomfortable for me and those around me.

Many times, I would drive back to the main base pissed, alone, and really not happy about who I was showing up as professionally and how it was affecting my social life. I wasn't in a good place nor was my team. Thankfully, we still got our missions completed but damn were we miserable.

The bright nights and days bled together. Never in my life had I been at such a low point emotionally, socially, and professionally.

One morning, while working with the Kiwi Air Force troops (six people counting the lieutenant) and a couple of my team members, I was feeling incredibly stressed out. We needed to get several very sensitive and expensive pieces of cargo properly secured to aircraft pallets, loaded on the trucks, transported to the airstrip, and loaded on skids ready for a C-130 bound for the South Pole. All by 1 p.m.

Collectively, we were dragging ass. It was hard to properly secure the pieces of the telescope (which would be used to measure black matter in space) without damaging them. And not damaging them was so important that a representative from the manufacturer had to be onsite while we secured them. This added huge amounts of time to an already tight schedule.

"Let's go. Let's get that secured and up on the truck. You need to be out of here in ten minutes," I barked to my team members through my face mask. My barking was met with no real change in work speed or intensity.

I scrambled over to the area where the Kiwis were working. "Lieutenant Biggins, how much longer will your troops be on those three pieces of cargo?" I asked, with hurried respect.

"We'll have them on the truck and ready to be out of here in about thirty minutes. Can you get someone on the forklift to load them in fifteen?" she asked.

The lieutenant had hardly finished speaking before I turned and started yelling across the work area at one of my workers. "Hey, get that forklift ready to lift these pallets on to the truck!"

No response from any of my people.

Without thinking, I screamed the command again. "Hey. Get that fucking forklift ready to lift these pallets!" Everyone stopped working and looked up in my direction. Almost in unison everyone shrugged their shoulders as if to say, *Fuck him*. Stunned by the lack of movement and response, I yelled, "Fine, I'll do it myself." I continued to mumble to myself as I went behind one of the huge cargo trucks toward the forklift. I hadn't noticed Lieutenant Biggins following behind me until she said, "Hey, Mike?"

Out of sight from the group, I stopped and turned, a rude retort on my tongue. I didn't have the time for this. But when I turned around, she was on me and up in my face. I backed up against one of the large cargo truck tires, stunned.

Her finger was pointed directly at my face. She was flushed either from the cold or she was really mad.

Then she let me have it.

"Listen, you fuck, you are an arsehole. I hate working with you and your team. My troops do not want to work with you or your fucked-up team that YOU made. You aren't a 'lead.' You aren't capable of leading anyone. You make this work horrible and hard when it shouldn't be. The other teams are far better to be around, and you are to blame. You have been a fucking arshehole."

She wasn't done.

"You are only halfway through this season and I don't think you are gonna make it. You get the job done but you bark at your people. You are a hard worker but you make it all harder than you need to. For everyone. You need to figure this out."

At this point, she was so close I could smell her breath.

"If you don't change your attitude and *lead* this team, I am gonna kick your arse!"

She hung her face in front of mine for an extra moment for extra effect. And it worked. I was scared.

She finally took one step back and turned to walk away, while tossing out a final comment. "Get your head out of your arsh. Start by apologizing to your whole team and my troops. That's the first step, you fucking arsehole."

She walked away leaving me pinned to the tire. I was amazed at the whole experience. Not only did I get my ass handed to me but I knew she was right. "Holy shit, she is good," I thought as I walked to the forklift.

Thankfully, the C-130 was delayed from the South Pole so we finished the mission that day on time.

The remainder of the day, and into the next, I was pensive and quiet.

Lieutenant Biggins was right. I had to apologize to the group, take my licks, and ask for forgiveness. I committed to myself that I would do this at the start of the next workweek.

Throughout the weekend I thought about how I interviewed so well for the cargo position only to set myself up for a horrible fall when I took it. I was so cocky and sure of myself then, acting with little self-awareness or regulation. Then I got here and my usual empathy and social skills had gone down the toilet, as I struggled to stay above water in the unpleasant mess I'd dived into. The level of emotional intelligence I'd been operating with was pathetic. I knew it was time to pick myself up, apologize and own up to my failings, give the team an opportunity to vent, and ask for forgiveness. From there we could start to rebuild our team.

I didn't sleep well over the weekend. I knew I was a far better leader than I had been showing up as. I was ready to start anew, clear the air, and lead.

When Monday came, I was glad of it. At the start of the first shift, I called together the Kiwi group, my team, and my supervisor, Bear. I asked everyone to get comfortable, saying, "I have something that I ask you to hear."

I *asked* them to hear on purpose. I wanted them to see I was changing the way I was leading, from that moment.

I looked everyone in the eye and then I got started. "I am asking you to hear what I have to say. Since our very first day together, it was obvious I was unqualified to be a lead cargo handler. A fact that many of you are rightly mad about. That fact caused me to revert to nonleadership behaviors most of the time and especially in already-stressful situations. I have barked, yelled, and given horrible directions to each one of you on many occasions. I have not been a good leader. I would not even call it 'leading.' Each one of your efforts has helped us to complete our missions. My asshole behaviors have made a hard job in harsh conditions far harder than it needed to be."

I paused to look at each person in the eye, which was very uncomfortable, but the situation called for it. Then I continued. "Going forward I will do my best to be a real leader. I ask that you forgive me and help me make our final time together better and our team better. I also ask that if anyone wants or needs to say something in order to move forward, please do so." It was quiet. "Now would be a good time," I added, with a bit of levity to release some of the tension I felt in me and in the large cargo bay.

The silence was only betrayed by the heater fans clicking on and blowing warm air into the bay. I continued to make eye contact with the group.

More silence. Then the oldest man in the room, both in years and time on the ice, stepped forward. His name was John.

"Mike, I appreciate what you had to say. I want you to know that I never liked working with you… until today. Thank you. Apology accepted." John stepped back into the group while holding his hat in his hand.

"Thank you, John," I said in a sober tone.

Then the most vocal member of my team stepped forward. She was a large woman who commanded attention. She was red in the face, and before she spoke I thought, *Oh boy. Here it comes.*

Surprisingly, she started off quiet. "I have been coming here for four years. I liked every year but—" and here her voice became louder and her face more flushed—"I *hate* coming to work now. I blame you. I blame you for making it suck. You're an asshole to work for. You yell and don't know what you are saying most of the time 'cause you just read it off the sheet. Stop being a dick! That's all. I am done."

Again, I said, "Thank you."

My go-to teammate, sitting on a box, said simply, "Thank you, Mike. Apology accepted. That must have been hard to say. But it needed to be said. Thank you."

A couple others said basically the same things. And as they did, the air in the room changed from uptight and cluttered with bad vibes to a bit more open, with possibilities.

Finally, Lieutenant Biggins came forward and said, "Thank you, Mike. How can I help move us forward as a team?"

I was surprised at the question, but I honestly answered. "Let me know if I can do something better." I turned to the group. "And I ask that from all of you. Please let me know if I can do something better to make your time here better."

I knew it was time to wrap it up and get to work. "For those who have not spoken up, no problem. Just know that I am going to do my best to be a better leader," I said. "Thank you for your help."

With that we finished the meeting.

A huge relief came over me. I felt the best I had felt since my comment about the chain, months prior. I had stopped the free fall.

I'd taken my first step toward being a better leader, and I felt relieved and energized.

Bear pulled me aside. "Hey, Mike. Good job. I appreciate you standing up for what everyone has been experiencing. That took some courage. I'm also glad you said what you did about being a lead. It's true, you shouldn't be a lead. But you're a hard worker. Now it's time for you to put it all together. Let me know how I can help."

"Thank you, Bear. I appreciate you. Thank you for not firing me. Seriously, thank you."

Bear let out a big belly laugh. "We don't fire people down here. That would suck." He turned and headed to the coffee machine with a chuckle.

From that point on, I continued each working day as an emotionally intelligent servant leader to my group. Asking myself, *How can I help? What is important to them for the remaining weeks on the ice?*

A key moment came when it was announced that in the near future several of my crew could begin flying with the cargo to different locations, remote and historic places like "Wiess Divide" and the South Pole. It was up to me who could go.

The custom was for the lead to go first and then the rest of the crew would follow as the schedule allowed. But during our morning meeting with the team, I stated I wouldn't go until everyone in my team had the opportunity to go first.

This was a big deal. Who doesn't want to go to Wiess Divide, a location so remote only a small handful of people on the planet ever experience it? The South Pole? Hell yes. I am all about it. But I knew this was important for the group, and my team appreciated my approach. We agreed on a system to select who got to go where. And it all worked out for the team. Except for me—I never got the chance to go to either location. Honestly, though, I am proud that I didn't go. Putting all my team members on the planes to savor those life experiences was the right thing to do. It's the kind of leader that I am (at least when I'm centered and congruent).

Our team began to perform very well. Everyone had their "thing to do," did it well, and we supported each other. I would say if there were badges, awards, and trophies in the cargo department on the ice, we would have won "the most improved team" award. I was proud of us. And I think they were proud of the work they accomplished.

Slowly my social life improved. First, I was asked to play checkers and Uno. Then I was taught how to knit and purl. I was even asked to join the "stitch and bitch knitting group." Basically, this group of mostly women drank wine, knitted, purled, and talked ("bitched") about everything. That group was a highlight of my experience on the ice. I really enjoyed—and still do enjoy—knitting and purling. (I was able to start and complete a baby's blanket for my great friend's firstborn. It turned out all right. Although it was more of a table runner than a blanket.)

I was also invited to parties and TV series groups, I wrote a newspaper article about working in Iraq and coming to the ice, and I was asked to make a presentation to the McMurdo Station about my experience in Mongolia with the Kazahks golden eagle hunters.

Soon it was spring, and time to leave the ice.

I finished my time there in a far better state than I came in. As difficult as it was, I was grateful for the hard lesson.

Emotional intelligence is the ability to experience, gauge, and manage your emotions at the moment that they are happening. Once I failed so deeply in this regard, I realized how truly important it was.

An emotionally intelligent leader will always check themselves before making a judgment, making a call, or taking action. And that is a truth I know I'll never again forget.

CHAPTER 6

New Zealand and Australia: Optimism

AFTER A LATE night, the morning comes up quick, and it's not entirely easy to pull myself from my warm bunk. But I climb out anyway and pull on fresh clothes. Then I busy myself getting packed and go to "put the kettle on." (The Englishman is starting to wear off on me.)

After breakfast today, we're heading downstream to the lower camp where Ian will do his twenty-four-hour solo, so we'll be closing up the cooking shack on our way out.

Ian comes downstairs to join me, and we take a few "vitamin I," or ibuprofen, to knock off the hair of the dog. Then we spend an hour cleaning, buttoning up the camp, and returning the "bear protection" plywood and Pine-Sol containers to the various doorknobs and windows.

I check that I turned off the propane, twice.

Satisfied, we close up and begin our hike—with a little extra ease. While here, we drank one bottle of the good scotch I'd packed in and eaten from my backpack like kings (sometimes). And we've now got considerably lighter packs as our reward for good behavior.

Ian and I make our way through the river valley, and soon we come to a fast and wide river bend. Resting on my pack, I wait for Ian to catch up. I hear him getting closer with every jingle of his bear bell, and I chuckle as he draws near.

"Bloody hell, man," Ian exclaims as he stops beside me and takes in the river ahead. "How are we going to get around that?"

"We aren't," I reply matter-of-factly. "We're going to ford the river together."

Ian takes a deep breath and raises his eyebrows.

"Let's eat now," I say. "We'll have some water and make a plan to cross the river."

I open the top of my pack and reach in for my bag of GORP— good ol' raisins and peanuts. "I want us well fed and watered once we get across so we can just keep moving toward the cabin. That water is cold and if we stop on the other side to eat and then the weather changes, we could be in for a long, cold rest of the day."

"Right." Ian continues to look at the river. "You really think that it's safe to cross the river here?" he asks as he rummages through his pack for food.

"Yep," I say, resting comfortably.

Ian is quiet. After a few minutes, he asks in a rough way, "How?"

"Ian, I think you're looking at our crossing the river pessimistically, as if it's a problem that's really difficult to solve. And that makes it more difficult. Instead, just eat your lunch and while you do so, do your best to look at our crossing the river not as a problem but something that will inevitably work out. Look at it through the lens of an optimist. And then just hold the intention to find the answer you know exists."

He snorts in laughter as he chews his sandwich. "Fucking hell, Mike. You sound like a ninja master or something."

I laugh a bit with him and then say, "That, my friend, is why I am a Master Coach." Still chuckling, I add, "Try it for a couple of minutes."

As we sit in quiet, the sun moves behind the clouds. Soon we'll begin to get chilled from the light breeze coming from upstream. I don't want us to cross the stream already cold; we need to get moving. So I stand up and start to coach Ian through looking at the situation from a place of optimism. "OK, Ian, where is the water moving fast?"

Ian points at the right side of the river as it curves around the bend.

I nod. "Right. We want to avoid that area. It's fast and deep. Not good." Then I ask, "Where can you see the bottom of the river on this side and the other side?"

Ian points in front of us, toward a slight angle upstream.

"Great," I say. "We will start and end there for the first point. Then we'll do the same on the other side of the bend. We'll get down to the river, undo the waist buckles on our packs, and walk single file, you holding my pack. We'll go at an angle upstream, with you staying right behind me. Since I'll be taking a lot of the pressure of the moving water, you'll have less to fight against. If you lose your footing, simply dog paddle at the same angle until you reach the natural incline of the other side. OK?"

Ian looks at me and then at the river. "Yeah, OK. But how is getting wet up to our waists and possibly swimming with this heavy pack on my back seeing this optimistically?"

I laugh and say, "I'll tell you on the other side. For now, you can also look at it this way—when we hit the other side, we'll be far less hungover than we are now. The cold water will wash it right away."

Without missing a beat Ian says, "Now that is optimistic."

We cross the river just as we'd laid it out, with no issues, to the farthest edge of the downstream side of the bend. As we quickly sit down on our packs and wring out our socks, I explain to Ian what I meant about looking at the situation from an optimistic point of view.

"When you came up to the bend, what did you see?" I ask.

"The river and a steep side," he says, as he puts on his right boot.

"Right. Did you see it as an obstacle?"

"Yeah, kind of. I saw it as something I wanted to go around so I didn't have to get wet."

"Exactly," I say. "And being focused on this, you might have wasted time and energy bogged down in your negative associations around getting wet, or searching for a solution to a problem that isn't really the point. You might have limited the range of your mind in exploring possibilities. Now, if instead you came up to the bend and just said to yourself, what is the answer to getting to the other side? Then what would you have done or thought?"

"I would probably just accept that getting wet was going to happen or not really think about it. Then I would start looking for where to safely cross."

"Right. Your mind would open to look for possibilities. You'd be more likely to see and evaluate the strength of the current, the bend, and where you could see the sides of the river. See? Optimism versus pessimism," I say.

"Well, I'm not hungover anymore," he says, finishing his left boot laces.

"So there's that," I say. "And keep trying to center in that optimistic viewpoint as we hike. You might be surprised how it allows you to see and experience things differently. In a wider way."

"I'll try," Ian says. "It would be easier, though, if you first tell me there'll be a fireplace at the cabin where I can dry my socks. Can you give me this foundation of optimism to build on or do I have to start with nothing?"

I laugh. "Yep, there's a fireplace. With lots of wood."

"Great. Let's get on with it then."

As we make our way toward the camp and promised fireplace, we pass near Egil's Knob, and the day's conversation with Ian suddenly tangles up with my memories.

Memories of proposing to my wife, Erin. Memories of boarding a plane to New Zealand together on Christmas Day, to live out of a van as we toured the North and South Islands for almost six months while I flew back to Oklahoma City every three weeks to provide on-site "land rig coaching" on the oil rigs. Memories of when I had my own lesson of optimism imprinted deeply on me for the first time.

Before I left Iraq for Antarctica but after my fateful interview, I'd been introduced (through a "Cigar Night on the Deck," a tradition I'd happily initiated) to two men from a leadership and training company, who were at the base on a consulting trip. We became fast friends and they offered me a job working for them as a leadership and communications facilitator, for what were mostly oil and gas companies around the world. I said thank you but no thanks—I'd just accepted a job in Antarctica for the following fall. I told them, though, that when I got back, I'd give them a call. And I did.

That move opened up a new sense of passion and purpose for me, as I began my first work as a leadership coach.

I started out by traveling around the United States, Africa, and Europe facilitating interactive leadership and communication workshops in the name of "creating a more efficient and safe work environment." I was successful and well commended in the role.

Then while in a Lubbock, Texas, in a Holiday Inn conference room, I had a conversation with a drilling superintendent named Tom, a humble, influential, and deeply respected man from a large land-based oil company. The conversation changed my life.

Tom told me I was good at what I did, and that I should take "this stuff" out to the rigs. Coach them right there, standing on the iron floor, right where it matters.

I valued this man's opinion and thought about his words for a moment. I asked him, "How would I do that—get onto the rigs and coach these guys?"

Tom grabbed his can of chewing tobacco from his jeans back pocket and smiled a small smile underneath his mustache. "Shit. Start a company," he said.

I just stared at him for a few moments. "I wouldn't even know where to begin," I stammered out.

Tom shrugged his shoulders as if putting on a coat, and said simply, "I'll help you."

And he did. I got my EIN number from the feds and the rest is history. Pretty great history, too—but not the very greatest.

The most defining history had already been made a few months prior, on December 29, 2009, around 11:30 a.m., when I met Erin and our story began—a mad, crazy, and supportive love that continues to expand and incapacitate the stuff of myth.

Our first date was the first day of the new year, I started my business that spring, and then we got engaged at the top of Egil's Knob, Alaska, under a full moon in late September. We rode out of the bush on horseback for two days. Then a few months later, we arrived in Auckland, New Zealand. It was my second time there, and Erin's first.

Erin immediately picked up on the laid-back feel of the

country. We spent a couple days hanging out in Taupo, a cool, easygoing town on a lake, waiting for our Kiwi friends Chris and Lindsey to introduce us to the van they bought on our behalf. Then we'd all drive, in our separate vans, to the Coromandel Peninsula for the New Year's celebration campout.

When Chris and Lindsey arrived in the white diesel Toyota Hiace 4x4 van, it was almost completely "kitted out," with a queen-sized bed, stuff for sleeping, storage space underneath, pots, pans, silverware, two chairs, a folding table, and tinted windows. Lindsey even made us curtains for the windows. The van was definitely "sweet as" (in other words, awesome, as the Kiwis say). Erin named the van "Pearl." And Erin and I were over the moon for Pearl.

Soon we were off, headed north to the Coromandel Peninsula on the busiest New Zealand holiday weekend of the year. The roads, gas stations, stores, and towns were packed. But everyone was still easygoing, eager to talk at the counter while paying for gas, and helpful at the stores. There wasn't any sense of "hurry up," "let's go," or "get out of my way" on the highway.

We spent the holiday weekend with Chris and Lindsey's friends. It was paradise, and we noticed how everyone seemed to be optimistic about everything. Even when it was pissing down rain, they like to say, "It's just a shower."

After the weekend, we started exploring, just the two of us, and Pearl.

The more time we spent in Pearl, the more we learned her quirks and started to figure out our systems—systems to keep the mosquitoes out of the van, systems for ventilation, systems for getting our gear in and out quickly and efficiently, systems for making, cooking, and cleaning up dinner. In time, we had a long list of areas where we needed to make improvements.

One day, we were headed out on the dirt road to the nearest town hardware store. Erin was driving.

It was nerve-racking for several reasons. It was Erin's first time driving on the "wrong side" of the road. There was enough traffic combined with narrow lanes that we'd often have to pull over or back up to find a passing point. Plus the road was full of sharp tire-eating rocks and we didn't have a spare. We made it to the store, but not without my stress level being at the max. Which did not make for a fun drive. For me, at least. Erin, hell—she was having a great time.

We found the hardware store full to the brim with people buying everything from a screwdriver to ice. The employees there were happy to help us find a lot of "the bits and bobs" we needed. If they didn't have them, they called around and asked other stores. But still no spare tire could be found, which kept me worrying. I lit a cigar and hoped that would help.

As Erin drove us back, she commented, "There aren't a lot of signs here saying, 'don't do this or that.' Just signs giving information."

Between draws on the cigar, I asked, "What do you mean?"

"You know," she said. "In the States there are usually signs that tell you what not to do. No overnight camping. That sort of thing. Here the signs are more like how to get somewhere."

"Yeah, you're right. Kiwis have got it together," I said. "I think their motto is"—I switched into my best Kiwi accent—"you do your thing as long as your thing doesn't affect mine. Don't be a dumbass."

Erin laughed as she shifted Pearl into a lower gear to start down the hill.

I was joking, but the more time we spent in the country, the better understanding we developed of the culture, and it felt pretty spot on. Most everyone was friendly, optimistic, and capable. It was like being around a bunch of fun, lovely MacGyvers, and we loved it.

Erin and I began to get into a rhythm. We'd get up, stretch, then drive to get coffee and tea. While drinking it, we'd decide what we wanted to do that day. We'd drive, make or buy lunch, drive a bit more, and find a place to camp for the night, either a campground with showers or right on the beach. When we stopped for the night, we'd unload the table, chairs, and stove. I would set up our "kitchen area" and Erin would uncork the first bottle of wine. We would sit, fight off the mosquitos, make a fire, and look at the sea. Later we would make dinner of chicken breast, salad, baked beans, and a vegetable, and uncork the second or third bottle.

This was our standard. It worked well with the lifestyle and feel of New Zealand. It also made our time fly, and soon it was time for me to return to the States for the first time to work. I'd be working three weeks on and three weeks off for most of the next six months. When I was gone, Erin would travel around in Pearl on her own.

My time working on the drill rigs always felt longer and more arduous than the time spent traveling around with Erin. For obvious reasons. Yet the level of contrast that emerged was still surprising.

I would spend at least twelve hours a day "on location" (at the drill site) "standing on iron"—in other words, on the rig floor working with the crews. Basically, my job was to offer coaching to a nine-man rig crew around leadership, communication, and problem-solving. Most of the time I was assigned to a rig that was known to have or did have "issues."

These issues came in many different forms. Possibly a lead driller with a "bad attitude" that had caused issues with the "company man" (the representative of the company that hired the drill company). Or maybe the rig had "issues with safety or being productive" or the rig had gone through a lot of workers quitting.

My job was very difficult for many reasons. The biggest reason, though, was that no one wanted me around. In fact, my first day back from Auckland I started on a rig with a man named Chris (also called "Toolpusher"), who I seriously thought might try to kick my ass in greeting. He rushed toward me, got in my face in front of all his men, and said, "What the fuck are you going to teach me about drilling or leading my men?" You could feel his anger in the air.

I told him, "Well, Chris, from what I understand, you put your men first. You care for them and protect them from the bullshit of the office. All that I'm here to do is help you do that even better and be able to teach it to your men so they can do it, too. It'll help them throughout their careers. Also, I don't know fuck all about drilling."

Chris was still in my face after I had finished. The smell of his Copenhagen tobacco made me want to take a step back, but I didn't. "Ha. You fucks from the office always want something," he said. "Stay the fuck away from me and my men."

Still standing face to face, I told him, "Sorry, Chris, I can't do that. I'm here to help you teach them what you know and then some. We're assigned together. Nothing I can do about it. Either way, I'm here as long as it takes. It's up to you to decide that. I'm just here to help you and your men."

Still not happy, Chris went into his office, grabbed a chair, and slammed it down on the ground. "Fine, this is where you will sit then." His men were shuffling with laughter.

"That's fine, Chris. However, I need my safety briefing from you about the location." Getting tired of the act, I threw out a request. "Can I please be part of our crew change safety meeting?"

Chris stared at me, then replied, "Nope."

I'd been looking for a place to stop the conversation where he and everyone listening could understand that I wasn't going anywhere and that I was there to help the crews. This was a moment to do so. "OK, Chris. I would hope in time that I'd be invited to attend. Later I'll ask you what I need to do to become part of the meetings and crews. However, it's not the time now. These men either want to get home to their families or start their hitch. I'll sit down in that chair until you're ready to give me the location safety brief."

Chris, satisfied with the draw, instructed one of his men to park my truck and, "Let's get this safety done. We'll meet up ih the change house."

With that the men who had just finished their hitch remembered they should be headed home, especially as no ass kicking was going to take place. So, they began to move about and jabber about themselves. I sat down in the chair and waited. A long time.

It was a waste of time, prompted by Chris's extreme pessimism. A pessimism that contrasted starkly with the other world I was engaged in, the optimistic Kiwi world. Both "worlds" had cultures, and the mindsets of each affected the outcomes of their day-to-day operations or experiences.

Chris's pessimism clouded his ability to fully lead his men. In fact, it affected his men in a negative way. The recent safety and production incidents they'd had proved this point. My job was to work with him on his leadership skills, and it was clear his negative outlook would need to be addressed.

I didn't start out that job as the most die-hard optimist myself. I certainly wasn't living like Chris, but interestingly, when I first arrived in New Zealand with Erin, the "optimistic" culture didn't always line up with me well. I found myself too on edge and overly focused on what-ifs, reaching our goals, and keeping the van in good working order. All of this kept me from really being able to take in the full experience, and caused for some friction with Erin and me.

Part of what helped shift my outlook came from a New Zealand tattoo artist named Andy. Prior to meeting Erin, I knew I wanted to get a complete sleeve tattoo representing my global experience of the "beauty of travel." I spent several years thinking of what I wanted, where, and why, and about the agelessness of the symbols that would live forever on my arm. I also spent a lot of time researching and interviewing artists. After Erin and I decided to take this trip, I focused my search on Kiwi and Aussie artists. I figured I'd find a world-class artist there, and have them start and ultimately complete my tattoo as I traveled back and forth from the States. When I interviewed Andy, we hit it off right away. A date was set to meet in Christchurch, New Zealand, for the first session.

When the time came, Erin and I rolled into the beautiful Christchurch downtown area midday. We met Andy at his home that evening for dinner. That night, we would "camp out" in his driveway and start the first tattoo session at his studio the next day.

Erin and I both got along with Andy, who besides being incredibly talented, had a "sweet as" nature and contagious sense of humor.

I was overjoyed with my first day in the chair. The start of the piece was beyond my wildest expectations. We stayed with Andy again that night, and much like the one before we shared a lot of laughter, stories, and wine.

Erin and I traveled around for a couple more days, and then I flew back to Oklahoma City to return to my work with Chris and his team. It was tough moving from the sunny vision of the Kiwis back into the atmosphere of the rig, but as I gave my word to support the "turnaround" of Chris and his crews, I knew I would keep at it. Erin returned to traveling around in Pearl.

Two days later, an earthquake with the magnitude of 6.3 caused severe damage in and around Christchurch. Our friend

Andy's life, and the lives of many others, changed forever. Half of Andy's studio collapsed, and his friend, a fellow tattoo artist who worked just down the street, died in the rubble of his own studio.

In time, I reached out to Andy offering my condolences. I followed his Facebook threads and knew he was busy providing water, food, and help to others. He also spent a lot of energy arranging for supplies to be brought into the city for weeks afterward. I wasn't surprised by his leadership and compassion for others, even while experiencing his own pain.

Meanwhile on the rig, I was making gradual headway with Chris and his team. I'd been allowed to join meetings, stop the job to ask questions, and even sit in Chris's office with him. About once every two days I would ask Chris a well-thought-out question about his leadership qualities or philosophy. I would never push him for an answer.

One day I said, "I would be curious to understand how you became a leader that each one of those men would do anything for." Then I let him think on it. It seemed an important question for him to sift through. Especially because I doubted he thought much about his strengths as a leader.

Chris's attitude of himself was a direct reflection of his leadership style—he always downplayed his influence, abilities, and stature. I decided that I would help Chris see how his self-deprecating thought process directly affected his crews and operations. Thankfully I was smart enough to know that our relationship was not strong enough yet to ask those tough questions.

I always did my best to leave Chris and the crews happy that I was with them for a few weeks. Or at least not mad at me.

To show total transparency I would ask Chris to read my report before sending it out for his supervisors to read. And since as a leader, Chris excelled at a number of things, I described this in the reports. I wrote the reports in a matter-of-fact way. With no frills, no big words. Just the facts. This resonated with him. It was the beginning of changing Chris's perception of himself.

I left that session on a high note, but I was still mentally exhausted. I didn't know it but my next interaction with Andy and those around him would change my perception and outlook in a powerful way.

I arrived back in New Zealand to find Erin waiting for me with open arms. After a couple days of hiking, we were going to head north to meet with Andy for the second session for my sleeve tattoo. Tattoo artists from all around New Zealand and Australia had offered Andy a space in their tattoo parlors for free so that he could still make a living, so Erin and I simply planned to follow him around as he completed my sleeve over the next three months.

When I first saw Andy I was taken by both how sad he was and also his positive attitude about "getting on after the shake-up." He had lost a friend while at the same time losing his studio. Yet he still was positive about "things working out." He was still optimistic for the future.

After finishing my session that day, Erin and I were out driving Pearl. When we were approaching a fork in the road, I asked Erin, "Which way do we have to go?"

"I don't know," she replied.

The fork in the road was coming up soon. And I like to know where I'm going, both while driving and in life.

"Well, you better find out," I said. By the strength and urgency of my directive you would have thought a life-or-death decision was about to take place.

"I don't know!" Erin said again.

I huffed and cussed as I turned into a parking lot, where I promptly lost my shit. "What the hell. You're the copilot. You need to know where we need to go to get us where we are going!"

I continued to go off, until Erin interrupted me. "What does it matter? We can simply turn around and go the other way! Why are you so intense about so many little things? It will work out. God, you are so agro."

And instantly, I knew she was right. I felt it like a ball-peen hammer between the eyes.

I felt ashamed.

I had blown up over a simple decision to turn right or left. When not two hours before I'd left an artist and friend who had suffered a real tragedy, losing his studio and someone he cared about, yet he was still finding a way to be optimistic about life. And I was huffing and puffing because the woman I loved added two minutes to our drive.

I sat silently, waiting until I had the right words. "I'm sorry, Erin. I don't know why I always need to know everything. I still have a lot to learn about remembering that everything will work out and that it's 'sweet as.' I'm sorry I yelled at you. I'll do better."

Erin answered abruptly. "OK. You don't have to be such a jerk about it. Let's enjoy this together."

By "this," I knew she was referring to our life.

We sat in the parking lot for a while in silence.

I silently promised myself to focus on "this," our life, as a Kiwi would. With optimism and the outlook Erin and I knew as "sweet as."

Erin and I continued to travel about New Zealand while I focused on the "sweet as" mindset. When I did, I saw and experienced many examples of things working out when I let go of my need to worry or control the outcome. Interestingly, the better I got at looking for the "sweet-as moments," the deeper the experience.

Each time I returned back to the rig, my attitude was noticeably more easygoing. Someone in New Zealand had told us,

"Americans are overdriven." And I was no exception. But something had shifted in me that day in the car, and I was no longer as forceful about getting things done. I relaxed and allowed more space for things to unfold.

At first, I had always been doing my best to "effect change" on the drill site. Hell, I was hired to do so. I was being paid very well to do so. So a positive change was expected by my clients. But sometimes I would find myself being "pushy" around meeting my milestones, in a way that only set me and the crew back.

The more time that I spent in New Zealand and grew in my own optimism, the more impactful my performance coaching became with the crews. Things just happened as they should, by focusing on what went right. The crews responded in their own time with their own set of milestones, and I simply facilitated what was important to them. In time, we continued to build on the successes instead of the failures.

Before I'd been hired, Chris's rig had scored one of the lowest scores in an audit of twenty-five or more rigs. The audits measure many things, such as operational excellence (doing what you say you will do and documenting it), safety measures, nonproductive time, knowledge of the crew members' job responsibilities normally and during an emergency, and feet drilled per hour. My job as an on-site performance coach was to help Chris raise that score.

Three months after I arrived, Chris was following through on his promise to his guys to help them score within the top three rigs of the fleet. My developing an easygoing coaching rhythm and technique supported his drive to do so. I facilitated his plan to raise their score. One day I was working to help him help his crews better understand the operational plan for the day and next couple of weeks.

"I'll let them know the more they understand what the plan

is the better they will perform," Chris said, after spitting his chew into an empty Coke bottle.

Doing my best to ignore the nasty spit in the clear container, I said, "And what else should they know about the plan?"

"That if it ain't done there is hell to pay?" Chris said with a laugh. "No, I'm kidding… I don't know. Just do the fucking plan is what I want them to hear."

"Is that the best you can do, Chris?" I said.

"Fuck, man… What? What else do these guys need to know?"

Standing up to open the door to some air, I said, "What did you want to know when you were on the rig floor getting soaked in oil-based mud?"

Trying to be funny, Chris said, "When can I go to the house?" In other words, when could he get out of there. He laughed, and I laughed with him.

"That may be true," I said. "But what did you really want to know or need to know?"

Chris turned his head to the right to look out the window. He took another spit in his clear plastic container, then said, "I fucking wanted to know why we were doing this shit!"

He had it. "Great! Do they know the 'why' of the plan?"

Chris was growing tired of the questions. "Fuck if I know."

"OK," I said. "I can see you're ready to get out there and check things out. Would you be willing to try something new for today and tomorrow?"

Happy that the conversation was almost over, he stood up and looked like he would say yes to anything as long as he could then leave the room. "If I can get out of here and that makes you happy before you finish your hitch tomorrow, yes. What do you want me to do?"

"Would you be willing to ask a couple of your guys during

your rounds today and tomorrow why they are doing… whatever the hell they're doing?"

"Yes," he said. "I can do that."

"Great. Last question," I said, standing in front of the door. "If you ask your crews the 'why,' how will that help you help them be better at their jobs?"

"Fucking hell, Mike." Chris began slipping out of his Crocs into his work boots. "I guess I'll know then what they need to learn."

"Yes. That's true. And if you can help fill in the blanks for your crews, how will that benefit the whole rig?"

"Jesus, Mike. You said, 'last question.' And it's obvious. Why do I have to say it?"

"Because, Chris, if you say it then I'll be able to help you do it. I can't read your mind. Nor would I want to." I laughed.

"Good point. If I help fill in the blanks for my guys the rig will benefit overall because then when those fucks from the office come asking questions, we all know the answers and then they can leave us alone and we can drill baby drill. Now get the fuck out of my way."

As I stepped out of the office with him, I said in an upbeat way mostly for the irritation of it, "Wonderful, Chris. Tomorrow before I leave for my time off, let's talk about what you're finding out and how you'll 'fill in the blanks.' Deal?"

Chris stepped off the metal grate and gave me the middle finger. "Fuck off, Mike," he said as he headed out on his rounds.

"Well, that went well," I said loud enough for him to hear. He shook his head as he walked on. The next day we had our conversation and a high-level plan.

The following weeks in New Zealand and Australia were amazing. Having a more optimistic view of the world allowed for Erin and me to have a wonderful time even in trying conditions.

After meeting up with Andy for what would be my final session in New Zealand, Erin and I headed to Doubtful Sound for a sea kayaking experience. And what an experience it was, filled with misquotes, "no see um" bugs, and surf that was just below my comfort level as an experienced sea kayaker. If I hadn't earlier changed my mindset I wouldn't have had any fun at all. In fact, I would have questioned our guide's knowledge. But in the end we were fine and lived to tell the story. Which was a fun one. And once we made land, I was disappointed. I didn't want the experience to end.

I'd really started internalizing the truth that our mindset sets us up for our experience.

Soon we made it down to Sydney where I was to fly out, returning to the States. Erin would continue on, meet up with a friend, travel a bit more, and ultimately return to New Zealand for a couple more weeks before handing over Pearl to our friends to sell for us. Erin would meet me in Colorado shortly after that.

I returned back to Oklahoma eager to experience the progress Chris and his crews had made. I was greeted by Chris with a familiar "what's up." Which I took as a "great to have you back."

I found out that Chris and his crews had progressed as I predicted. Crew members that didn't have any time "for sitting around talking and learning about the different jobs on this location" were reassigned to other rigs or "the house" (fired). Those who remained did their jobs well and always looked to learn.

"This location has changed," Chris said while putting a huge dip of tobacco into his lip. "It's easier now than it was. Keeping it positive or at least being more positive is easier on the guys and me."

I sat quietly, waiting to hear if he would continue. He didn't. He just looked at me and spit into his clear plastic container.

Overlooking the container of spit, I calmly asked, "What

are the next steps now for you and your crew to be the highest performers in the fleet?"

In a matter-of-fact way, Chris answered, "Keep doing what I am doing. Teach these guys at each tour change, whenever I can, and have them teach each other."

Nodding, I said, "And if you continue to do this, what will be the result for you and your men?"

His eyes narrowed. "Those fuckers will see that we ain't a bunch of pansies down here."

"Great," I said. "You ain't gonna be a bunch of pansies. I like it. But think farther down the line for your guys. How will they continue to benefit?"

Chris paused and thought before he answered. "Well." He looked out the window. "If they continue to understand the what and the why we're doing things we are, they can continue to work up and be somebody in this shithole company."

I paused for effect. "Who will they remember for that?" I asked.

"Not me," he said anxiously, not wanting to take on any of the credit.

"Ah hell, Chris, they will remember you. You, the thorn-in-the-side-of-the-office-negative-asshole leader turning into a take-the-time-to-teach-them-the-what-and-why leader."

"That ain't me. Fuck it ain't," Chris said with another spit.

"Chris, it is. Those men love working for you. You put them first. Every day. You can sit here and deny it but it's true," I said. "I have a challenge for you. If you meet this challenge, I am done here. I'll head on down the road to the next rig location. Want to hear it?"

Grateful that the spotlight was off him, he said, "Yeah, what do you got?"

"You and I have three weeks together. During that time,

I would like to see you keep doing what you have been doing because it's working. However, I would ask that you also think about taking it to another level." I leaned forward. "Instead of looking at each situation or problem focused on the problem, instead focus on what could be the solution. If you do that, I think you'll be surprised at how your leadership style grows even more and the results will be at an even higher level. It's a small but powerful leadership skill. Can I have your permission to coach you around this during this last hitch?"

Chris leaned back to look out the window, then turned back to me. "If I let you coach me on this, you'll move on down the road to the next location after this hitch?"

"Yes," I said. "Remember in ten days our rig audit is taking place, so you need to get on this soon."

Chris tightened up at the thought of three office guys hanging out on the location for two days doing their audit. "Yeah, I guess. No matter what comes from the audit, you'll still move on down the road, right?"

"Yep. I'll tell Don my work here is done as long as you do your best."

"Fine, I will do my best to get you the hell out of here. Fuck, you are annoying to have around, most if not all the time."

Half laughing, I said, "I like you too, Chris. It's a deal. Three weeks looking at things as 'what is the solution' not 'what is the problem.' We will call this the 'sweet as' outlook. OK?"

Chris stood up, having had enough of this conversation. "Yeah. Whatever the fuck you want to call it. 'Sweet as' or 'sweet ass.' I don't give a fuck."

Getting out of his way so that he could get out the door, I got the last word in. "Ah, but you do, Chris, that's why you and your guys are doing so well. You do care. But don't worry," I said as he continued to walk away, his trademark middle finger rising. "I won't tell anyone. It's our secret."

Over the next week and a half Chris begrudgingly opened himself to the feedback and coaching. Small tweaks to his learned mindset of pessimism allowed one of optimism to begin to take shape.

The rig auditors came and went.

Chris's leadership continued to improve after the audit, too. He was noticeably more relaxed and proud of his men. He started more conversations with a question and was patient waiting for an answer. Four days before our hitch ended, the rig location superintendent arrived on location unexpectedly. Normally he would call and let Chris know he was coming first, so the sudden arrival put everyone on alert. The driller didn't even have time to give a quick toot on the rig horn as a warning to "not do anything stupid."

The superintendent stepped out of his truck holding a folder and sounding somber. "Chris, let's go inside and go over the findings of the audit. They wanted me to come down here and have a conversation with you."

Chris turned pale. "Sure. Come on in. You… you want coffee?"

I stayed where I was and let Chris pass to my right. The normally chipper superintendent said, "Yeah, I drove through the night to get here as soon as I could. I could use some coffee."

As he passed by me he gave me a wink and a smile as if to say, "I'm fucking with him. Watch this."

The superintendent stopped at the door and turned around. "Mike, you should stay outside for this. Go to the rig floor and tell the driller he's in charge. Don't bother us. OK?" He winked again.

"Yes, sir," I said.

A few minutes later, the rig floor phone rang. It was Chris telling the driller to stop operations, keep track of the pressures, and gather the men for a meeting.

Chris and the superintendent arrived in short order, both looking serious.

"Guys, I ain't one to fuck around or hold anything back," Chris said. "We got the results from the audit. You all did a good job doing what you know. I appreciate it. The super came all this way down from Tulsa to tell me personally."

No one moved. They all hung on his next words.

"Guys, we were at the bottom of the list for rigs in the fleet for doing stupid shit." Chris held on for a second or two more. "But now we are… number fucking three! We jumped nineteen rigs to get to the top three!"

We ate well that day and into the next. My client agreed that my work on the rig was completed. They asked me to return after my time off with hopes that through my coaching I could "do what you did with Chris and his crews on another rig."

I continued to work with other rigs for the next eighteen months, with each rig location turning themselves around and becoming high-performing, sustainable rigs. Soon the word got out and I was recruited into the Deepwater offshore business units off the Gulf of Mexico. There I would work on the drill ships, "coaching and standing on iron" in seven thousand feet of water.

As I continued to speak, work, and simply "be" from the heart as a coach to those I had the honor to work with, my client base began to grow.

Coaching came naturally, and I found that my coaching skills were useful, valued, and necessary in all industries, not just high-stakes industrial environments. I started being asked to work with a range of clients in various fields—engineering, hotel services, cybersecurity, aerospace. I even worked with a Montana dude ranch. Today, I have a very diverse portfolio of clients, all of which came to me by word of mouth.

The success I had on the rigs and in all my work going forward has been in part due to my coaching toward the leadership truth of optimism.

Leading with optimism supports leaders asking questions from a place of service. This place of servant leadership allows a leader to then create a space of learning and development within their people instead of encouraging a robotic do-this and then-do-that. Which requires no thinking and is, of course, when incidents happen.

Chris, like many in the high-stakes oil and gas exploration and drilling industry, initially believed that a command-and-control (pessimistic) leadership was needed and was the only way to succeed. Over the course of my time coaching Chris and others, I've been able to create a level of trust that lets them simply try another way. Once leaders experienced the results, they were more inclined to continue with optimistic leadership behaviors. In time, the whole location caught on, encouraging the sustainability of high performance throughout the crews.

Once optimism takes hold in one leader, things really change. I've experienced it in many high-risk industries and offices throughout the world.

And more importantly, I've experienced it in myself, in the most important area of my life.

It's a transformative truth.

CHAPTER 7

Africa: Legacy

IAN AND I make it to the camp (and its promised fireplace) in good time, just before sunset and its cold shadow.

The small but sturdy cabin is laid into a strand of flat land with plentiful trees, and the sight of it, like always, floods me with feeling. I've spent many days here living the "Alaskan bush life," and I feel at home. I imagine much like the man who cut down the trees to make this cabin sixty-plus years ago.

Ian is overwhelmed with the whole scene. Something about it seems to strike a chord in him, too.

He drops his pack and walks around, wet socks forgotten, his arms stretched out, palms forward, fingers totally straight, as if streaming the energy in and out.

"This place is awesome, Mike," Ian says with his arms still wide. "What's the history?"

"Let's get it ready for the night first. Then over dinner I'll tell you about it."

After we change out of our wet clothes and lay them out by a freshly lit fire, we get to work. While we sweep out the twenty-by-ten-foot interior, Ian continues taking in the cabin. "It looks like it has seven different layers of roofing, Mike. Look at the craftsmanship of these notches. And you can see that he planed out the floorboards by hand. Fucking hell, that is a lot of work," he says.

I uncover the two windows to let in some light and then we lay out our cots and bedding. Then I take the water container, pots, pans, and washing tubs outside. Ian gets some water from the river, we wash the pots and pans, and I make a makeshift table near the firepit.

The night is now cooling off, but—in dry clothes at least—the air still feels wonderful. Especially in the last few beams of direct sun.

We'll cook outside tonight. Soak it up as much as we can.

I light a fire and take out our Heather's Choice "meals for adventuring." Each one "made with love in Anchorage, Alaska."

As the water heats up to a boil, I pour the scotch and take out my travel cigar case. I remove two fine Plascencia cigars and begin to gently cut the ends, making sure to cut right at the shoulder. Then I start to tell Ian a little of the history he'd asked about.

"The cabin was built back in 1928 by a man named John Colvin. He was a commercial market hunter, which meant he basically hunted this valley for moose, Dall sheep, and other game, to supply meat to Healy and other towns along the railroad. Colvin got here midsummer or early fall, and then cut down the logs and built the cabin—as you noticed, with care and craftsmanship—before the snow fell that winter. He hunted out of it for years to come, and at some point he laid claim to this piece of land."

I pause to hand Ian a cut cigar, then light both his and mine with a wooden match. He nods his thanks. "The current owner is an outfitter named Coke Wallace," I continue. "An outfitter I spent a decade working for as a big game hunting guide. Which means I've spent a lot of time here. It's part of Colvin's legacy, but it feels like a part of my history now, too."

I finish the story with a draw on my cigar. The blue smoke escapes through my mouth and into the graying sunlight.

Ian sits quietly for a few minutes, sipping his scotch and puffing his cigar. Then he looks at me. "What do you feel your legacy is, Mike?"

I take the boiling pot off the fire, pour the water into the meal bags, and close them up to let them "rehydrate." "Ian, I will answer that question after you complete your twenty-four-hour solo that starts tomorrow morning. During which I want you to think about what your legacy is currently and what you want it to be in the future."

"Fair enough, I guess." Ian puffs out his question. "So how does tomorrow play out?"

"Well," I say, gently shaking the meal bags to make sure the water gets everything inside, "it's simple really. After an early breakfast I take you there—" I point over my left shoulder—"with everything you'll need. Food, which you can eat or not, water, a tent, whatever gear you want to take, a lighter, and a whistle."

Ian seems good with everything until the last item. "Whistle. Why a whistle?"

"For you to blow if you see a bear or something happens to you. Blow the whistle and I will come running. Basically, it's only for emergencies."

Satisfied with that, Ian recaps. "So you take me out there—" he points over my shoulder—"after breakfast, I stay out there with food that I can eat or not, water, camping kit, and a mighty 'whistle' for emergencies?"

"Yep, with a mighty whistle, but don't worry, you'll have your bear spray," I add with a wry smile.

"Great, fend off the bears with bear spray and a whistle."

"Yep, bear spray and a whistle!" I say happily.

Ian shakes his head and laughs, then continues. "So during this solo I sit, think, and journal about anything?"

"True. May I suggest something?"

Ian's face looks up. "Yes."

"Sit, think, and journal with the intention of mapping out your legacy given all your gained insights during our time together. Map out the how, who you will be, and the benefits for you, your loved ones, and those you lead. If you need to put in goals and timelines, go ahead. It's your solo."

Ian settles on more of a statement than a question. "And you will come check things out from time to time."

I reach forward to open up the meal bags. "Yep. But I won't say anything to you. If you need something, ask for it. But you shouldn't need anything."

I hand a meal bag to Ian. "Dinner's ready."

We eat, clean up, and finish the evening talking around the campfire. Once the fire dies out we head into the cabin to our awaiting cots. We're both tired. Lots of ground, both mental and physical, has been covered. Tomorrow will be a day to recover and reflect.

The next day, we wake, eat, gather up Ian's gear for the solo and head out "there," about 150 yards away from camp. Basically within "whistle distance."

I tell Ian in a matter-of-fact tone, "Here are your boundaries that I ask you respect for the experience." I walk over to a large tree and put my hand on it. "From this tree to that fat rock over there to that cluster of trees to that dead tree behind you. Don't pass over them. I'll come check on you in about two hours, then at lunchtime, dinnertime, and just before dark. You have enough food and water till tomorrow. I'll come get you in the morning."

As Ian looks around at his new home, I finish with a command. "Seriously, only blow your whistle if it's an emergency."

Irritated, Ian says, "Alright alright. Leave me be."

"Do you need anything?" I ask.

Ian is already getting his "solo camp" sorted. He says, "No, Mike. Don't you remember me telling you that I checked my kit twice? I've got all that I need, thank you. See you later."

"Well I leave you to your solo. Enjoy the experience." And with that I walk back to the cabin.

Twenty-four hours pass without one stray whistle and I pick Ian up in the morning.

He's both happy and serious. Most of my clients are after their solo.

We eat breakfast mostly in silence. I figure when Ian is ready to talk about his experience, he will let me know. We discuss the easy stuff like the weather, sleep, noises at night, and the day's plan. Which I tell him is, "An easy river crossing to gain a trail over the saddle into another valley with nice tent campsites. Our final campsite. With a five-hour day of hiking tops." Ian's keen on this part.

I've already broken down most of camp so that we can quickly eat and get on the trail to the final campsite.

We hike and rest in mostly continued silence to the camp without incident.

"This tundra is fluffy. Here is where the tent should go, Mike!" Ian exclaims like a small boy. "It will be better than all the mattresses I have slept on in my life."

Without looking I send a quip in his direction. "It will not be 'fluffy,'" I say, mimicking his British accent, "if you keep walking all over it."

"Cripes, Mike, why do you have to be so cheeky about it?" Ian laughs, stepping back away from the bed of moss. I'll go get water so that you can put up the tent. Don't want to screw anything else up as you finish setting up camp."

"Excellent. Fetch some wood while you are at it."

After a while all camp is set up and we're both pleased indeed. The campsite is about four feet above the creek, which allows for the rushing stream to be easily heard. We set up our firepit downstream, thirty feet away from our tent area. It makes a fine camp for our last night.

We finish dinner, clean up, fetch more wood, and enjoy the space. In time Ian starts the "real conversation" off with a statement. "You never answered the question, Mike."

"And what question is that, Ian?" I say.

He sits quietly for a few moments prodding the fire with a long stick, then looks at me. "What do you feel your legacy is, Mike?"

"I was just about to ask you the same, Ian. You beat me to it." I smile as I stand to put on a jacket. "But fair enough. We can let yours simmer just a bit longer. I feel my legacy is tied up in the life of travel, service, exploration, and seeking that I've lived, and how I pass that on to others in my work and carry it through my family."

"Hmm," he murmurs. "That's beautiful, Mike." He tips his glass at the trees. "Is it also tied to this place, Alaska?"

"Yeah, at least in part. There's something special about this place that's always called to me. It feels right to share it with my kids," I say. "If we're talking places and legacy, though, Africa might feel just as important to me."

"Africa?" he asks. "It's where this all really started."

I tell him about Ibn Battuta's book, and how his written legacy spurred me, a small-town young man, into a world of international travel. And into my own legacy. "He was born in Africa in what's now Morocco in 1304. And how he lived, and what he wrote— *The Rihlal: A Gift to Those Who Contemplate the Wonders of Cities and the Marvels of Traveling,* he changed the trajectory of my life," I say.

I think back to how the first three pages of his book made my heart race, my back straighten, and my soul expand to global possibilities. How it gave me the understanding that if I gave of myself, I could travel the world. It's what brought me here, sitting under the Alaskan sky.

I'm eternally grateful.

"His roots in Africa make the place meaningful to me. And the continent also holds my family's roots. It's where Erin and I spent our honeymoon," I tell him. "It's about legacy to me through and through."

We sit in the quiet of the crackling fire for a moment, then he gets up to find his jacket in his backpack near the tent. As he passes out of the orange glow of the fire and disappears into the dark, I think about experiencing Africa with Erin, as we began our own legacy, emerging from the commitments of our vows. It was the perfect place to start a life together.

A sense of legacy permeates our interaction with almost every aspect of the continent and its history.

It was Erin's dream to trek to and "sit" with the Bwindi mountain gorillas of Uganda and safari around the Ngorongoro Crater in Tanzania. So we built our honeymoon around that region of Africa, with the intention to experience all it had to offer. "It would be rude not too," Erin said. As part of this great adventure, we were also blessed to experience the dust and movement of the epic Great Migration on the Serengeti—which was unforgettable. Afterward, we came to rest in Stone Town, on the island of Zanzibar off the coast of Tanzania.

While all our experiences in Africa were epic and stunning, Stone Town stands out to me as the deepest embodiment of legacy. Its unique culture, history, and fantastic architecture bring to life a colorful, dark history and heritage. Because Zanzibar is smack dab in the trade winds of the Indian Ocean trade routes, it was accessible to traders and colonists from Arabia, India, Africa, Persia, and Europe. All these diverse influences come to life in its old streets and buildings.

On our terrace overlooking this historic city, we sat looking out at the Indian Ocean and the timeless dhow boats and talked about what we wanted to build together as husband and wife. I focused on the values we wanted to model for our kids. Erin focused on our living a rich life of experience. As the sun set that night, we agreed to live a life with our children that would teach them to be honest, hardworking, and adventurous. Their friends would call us the "cool parents." Somewhere between our third and fourth drink, before the sun fully slipped beneath the horizon and the dhow boats faded to black, we also agreed that our legacy as a family would be one of honest service and hard work on behalf of our fellow human beings, while living an adventurous, fun life to remember, centered on the outdoors bringing out the best of our bodies and souls.

I think of our boys, five and eight. I'm happy I can say Erin and I are giving them the life we talked about ten years ago. She and they are my biggest, best legacy by far.

This work I'm privileged to do is a great runner-up, though.

I take another sip of scotch as Ian walks back into the flickering firelight.

"Did you get lost out there?" I call over.

He comes to sit by the fire. "No. Just thought I'd take a minute. Figured you'd be asking some nosy questions soon and I wanted to think in peace first."

"Smart man. So, Ian, what is or what do you want your legacy to be now—with your family, your colleagues, and your community?"

He pauses, then smiles. "You know, I was thinking of that during my solo, and just now, but I still need to sit with it a bit more. It feels important."

"It is important. Just stay present with it."

"I will, Mike."

The light of the soft alpine glow finally fades from the tops of the mountains and darkness falls. We sit for a while watching the fire flash, snap, flicker, and send its warmth out past the rocks that contain it.

As the fire slowly burns out, the silence begins to be too much for Ian. (Mainly because I've been quiet for what feels like ten minutes.) He says, "You know, all of this Alaska experience and the solo has been great for me, Mike. I really needed it. For too long I did what I thought I should do. Not in fourteen years have I done something for myself where I could just be out and away from it all. I guess now we call it unplugged. Although I've been exhausted both mentally and physically at times out here, I've been able to recharge and sort things out."

Ian reaches for a stick to move a piece of wood farther into the center of the fire. Then he looks up and meets my eyes.

"Okay. My legacy. Maybe I still don't know the exact words for what I want it to be, but—I know my family, my marriage, and my health are most important. I've done well at times with some of that and other times I haven't done well at all. Too often I guess I've focused on what I thought was important and chased that 'thing' down a rabbit hole."

Ian takes a deep breath and looks into the fire. I remain quiet, not wanting to turn his attention from what he's reaching for.

The flames are starting to give off more light and energy, and when they reach their zenith, he speaks again. "In the end, I need to focus on those three things. Family, marriage, and health. If I do that, everything else will fall into place. Especially family. I know it. Because when I was out near that glacier calving, or in the heli for the first time, or when I was 'stepping into the scree,' or all alone with just my thoughts during the solo, I didn't think about work or my company or my country club mates. I just thought of my family."

Ian raises his eyes back to mine. "The other night in the upper cabin, your snoring woke me. I got up to take a wee and stepped out on the overlook, and when I sat down in the moonlight and looked over the valley with the trees and the moonlight, it was incredible. In that moment I thought, 'Wow, I wish my wife and kids could experience this.' It's a moment of beauty and realization that I will take to my dying day. Thank you, Mike. I really appreciate this. I really do."

I sit quiet for another couple of breaths, then simply say, "You're welcome, Ian."

After a few minutes, he stands up and says good night, then walks toward the tent. I stay behind just a bit longer to feel the gratitude.

Then I get up, put the fire to rest, and double-check the camping area. Satisfied, I walk to the tent, unzip it, and slip into my sleeping bag up to my rib cage.

I lie awake looking into the pitch darkness. Thoughts and images begin to play across my mind.

When in service to others, I realize, not only do you learn to give of yourself but you learn to simply say, "You're welcome."

Then images of my own path discovering my life truths start

to flash, and I see it all as my Hero's Journey. The excitement of "answering the call," the journey itself, a sense of warmth for the person who "set me straight" followed by a pang of gut-deep embarrassment or unease from learning the lesson. And in the end, here I am, in a tent in the bush of Alaska, reliving my truths of leadership. Courage, integrity, intention, emotional intelligence and awareness, optimism, and legacy. I see all the faces of those men and women I've had the honor of working with around the globe, and I feel a strong sense of service, honesty, gratitude, hard work, fun, and genuine generosity.

As I sink into sleep, I think how all of this, too, is part of my legacy.

We wake up rested and ready for the last push to the road. I'm ready to see my family and Ian is ready, as he says, "to get a call into my family, have a shower, some proper beer, and see someone other than your ugly mug."

I'll miss him, too.

We eat breakfast, leave no trace at the campsite, and take some final pics before putting on our packs. Ian naturally makes sure he has his bear spray with him before we head out into the river valley.

Our day starts out easy, being in a tight valley with multiple creek (pronounced "creeeek") crossings where we get our feet wet from the start. Then comes the hard final push where we've got to gain elevation out of that valley to the road. It's up, over, down, slog and slog some more, and then up again. I stay ahead a ways.

I stop to wait at the top of the long incline for Ian, who isn't far behind. In fact, he does a good job keeping up. As he arrives, he takes a look around. He looks down to the creek valley below and says, "Hell, we came all that way yesterday. That's amazing." He takes his pack off and sits down to rest.

Looking through my binoculars for game, I say, "How are you doing, Ian?"

"Alright, I guess. Getting on." He puffs out.

"Nice. You're doing great. In about twenty minutes we'll reach the top of the final hill. Then we cruise across the mountainside. There we can eat something before the last and final push. Sound good?" I say, still looking through my binos at some lambs and ewe sheep across the valley.

"Yep. No problem," Ian says.

Time passes and the sun comes shining directly down on us. I put my binoculars down to take it all in.

Ian pipes up, as we face toward the way we came yesterday.

"I've been thinking more about legacy this morning. Is it OK to also know what I *don't* want my legacy to be?'

I open my eyes, sit up, and direct my attention to Ian. "Sure, it can be whatever you want or don't want. It's yours."

"I don't want to work those long hours anymore. I want to be home some nights when my girls get home from school," he says, in a firm and strong manner. "I also don't want work to be chore or hassle. I want it to be fun." His face opens up with a smile. "I want work to be fun. Fun like our company Christmas parties."

Still giving my attention to Ian and sitting quietly, I smile and say, "And what else?"

"I don't want work coming home with me. I want to focus on those things that matter once I get home." He pauses with his head down. He starts to pick at the rocks. Then he goes silent for a long time.

The sun goes behind the clouds and a chill begins to build on my back. I stand up and put on my pack. "Ian, sounds like you are well on your way to understanding what your legacy is going to be both at home and work. I encourage you to think of how you'll know you are living that legacy. What it would look like or feel like to the others 'that matter.'"

I continue up the slight incline to the summit of the final "hill," leaving Ian to ponder the thought and in time walk to join me. I look back as I get to the top of the summit, thankful that it's behind us. I've always hated that incline but the view up the valley is amazing, and worth it. I continue to scan the horizon at the rugged beauty that I know from afar, up close and personally.

As we stop for lunch, we bask in the sun, and continue to speak about legacy for him and me. When he finishes sharing his vision, I simply ask him, "How will you stay true to it?"

Lying back against his backpack with his bear spray still within arm's reach, Ian says, "Come on, Mike. Stop with the questions! How about saying something like, 'Ian, if you really work hard, you'll be drinking a fresh pint in less than three hours! So come on, lad, buck up and get on the trail. Yeehaw!"

We both laugh. When I stop, I say, "It's funny when a Brit says yeehaw. It does not work, Ian. And back to your point about beer, I am not a bar guide. Just your coach. And soon we'll be at the road, where you'll turn on your phone and the world will come rushing back in again. So I'll ask you again, Ian. How will you stay true to it?"

"Right." Ian turns serious. "Back in those mountains somewhere I committed to be home two nights a week with my family and not to work weekends. I will hold myself accountable by stating this to my wife and the girls tonight on the phone and in my big upcoming meeting with my board of directors. That's the line in the sand." Ian's words are strong and firm.

Looking over to him, I ask one more question. "And what else?"

He stops walking and looks at me. "Mike, there is nothing else. That is it."

I simply say, "Great, Ian. As we get closer to the road, I want you to think about who will benefit if you do that, and what that will do for you, your relationships, and your career."

"I will," he says.

Ian looks over at the mountains to the south and notices a familiar distinct mountain peak. He puts two and two together. "Hey, we flew over this area. Right?"

"Yep," I say. "Let's get a move on."

Ian nods and we start walking again. "Hey, Mike, how and where did you find your own truths—about life and leadership?"

I pause at the question and think for a moment. "Great question, Ian. How about I tell you at the end of the trail while we wait to be picked up?"

"Agreed. I need a pint and I'm starting to get cold. *And* I know your answer will be long-winded, with lots of tales of adventure in faraway places. I'd better be sitting down."

I laugh at the truth of his answer. "Ah man, ain't that the truth. Let's go."

AFTERWORD

My intention with this book was to share my story of how a small-town fourth-generation railroader's son, through a chance encounter with a book, could go on to travel the world and find his deepest truths. I sincerely hope you found it entertaining and encouraging, and most of all, I hope you take something away from it that benefits you, those around you, and those you lead.

As I've continued to grow as an individual and a Master Certified Coach, I've come to believe that leaders are formed in the wild—where you go once you answer that "Hero's Journey call" and step from the known into the unknown.

In writing this book, I never set out to tell you what your life and leadership truths should look like. My truths might be similar to yours or they might be entirely different. Instead, I wrote this book with the hope that my experience might invite and empower you to answer your own Hero's Journey call to step into the wild and find your own truth of self, leadership, or life.

Many times friends, family members, strangers, and clients have said, "You should write a book. I would read it." For their encouragement, I am truly grateful.

Writing this book has been incredibly meaningful to me.

Firstly, I wrote for my mother; my wife, Erin; and my two

sons. I simply wanted to make them proud and leave a legacy of my experiences.

Secondly, I wrote for my past, present, and future clients, both virtual and face-to-face. Finding and living your truth allows everything else in life to flow. Once my clients find their truths, their lives begin to align and the sense of needing to force things starts to fall away, to the benefit of all around them. In this alignment, they build a legacy that matches their truths. Those like Ian, who have taken the step to schedule time with me in the outdoors for a global Adventure Coaching session, have chosen to unplug, do something for themselves, or recharge as they turn inward to look for these truths. But stepping into the wild can look like a lot of things. It can also happen in a conference room or over a series of Zoom calls. And I'm honored to share my story in a way that can support all of my clients' journeys. They all look different, but they're all powerful.

The "exercise" of writing has also been far more fulfilling on a personal level than I ever expected. Never did I—or my mother or my wife for that matter—think I could sit down long enough to type out the 110,000 words that made up my first draft! But I did it.

The act of writing has allowed me to reinforce my memories of life-changing people, incredible moments, chance encounters, trials, tribulations, lonely times, crazy times, drunken times, some flush-with-cash times but mostly poor times, and the breathtaking landscapes behind it all. Enriching tapestries of beauty, kindness, and life that in the end brought me to discovering my truths.

I'm honored to share it all.

ABOUT THE AUTHOR

Leaders are formed in the wild.

Mike Green is a transformational coach, author and facilitator who has worked with executives, professionals, entrepreneurs and thought leaders in 63 countries over 30 years. His unique methods including dynamic workshops, virtual coaching, face-to-face coaching, and adventure coaching help uncover the untapped potential within each leader.

From the awe-inspiring Altai Mountains of Mongolia to the Savannah of Africa, on the slopes of an active volcano in South America or the majesty of Alaska, Mike has an unparalleled ability to facilitate the personal development each leader must embrace to become great.

Mike Green is accredited as a Master Certified Coach by the International Federation of Coaches. He ranks in the top 1/10th of 1% of all coaches globally for his excellence, experience and knowledge. Mike works with individuals and organizations who want to banish mediocrity from their lives and embrace excellence. He lives in the interior of Alaska with his wife and two children.

If you are not already living life at your best and highest value to the world, this is for you.

Dear reader,

You'll never discover the truth about yourself behind a desk, but in the rugged wilderness of Alaska, on the breathtaking plains of the Serengeti or in the stunning Altai mountains of outer Mongolia.

Extreme environments challenge us to become the best version of ourselves by drawing upon the courage within each of us to achieve new levels of performance.

Mike Green will guide and coach you on a journey of self discovery and transformation based on his 30 years of experience helping other successful leaders to achieve goals ordinary coaches would claim are impossible. True…

Whether in group or individual coaching or customized travel expeditions, Mike Green can lead you up the mountain of self-discovery that every great leader in business, sports or military service must conquer before being transformed.

You will doubt yourself, but that doubt will be destroyed through determination and the realization that your doubts are just that.. doubts that you will conquer.

You will be tempted to quit, but that temptation will be transformed into a serene confidence.

You will begin with questions and answer them definitely as you discover the truth of the leader you were made to be.

Start your journey today with Master Certified Coach Mike Green by applying below:

www.MikeGreenLeadership.com/bookapply